PROBLEMS AND PERSPECTIVES IN HISTORY

EDITOR: H.F.KEARNEY MA, PHD

The Enlightenment

PROBLEMS AND PERSPECTIVES IN HISTORY

EDITOR: H. F. KEARNEY MA, PHD

Titles already published:

BRITAIN AND GERMANY BETWEEN THE WARS
ORIGINS OF THE SCIENTIFIC REVOLUTION
THE RENAISSANCE
THE DREYFUS AFFAIR
LOUIS XIV
SOCIAL CHANGE AND REVOLUTION IN ENGLAND 1540-1640
THE ENLIGHTENMENT
THE ORIGINS OF THE INDUSTRIAL REVOLUTION
THE ROMANTIC MOVEMENT

In preparation:

THE NEW DEAL 1933-1939
THE THIRTIES
THE MODERN EUROPEAN MIND
THE ORIGINS OF PARLIAMENT
THE RESTORATION
FROM BISMARCK TO HITLER
THE RISE OF CHRISTIANITY
CAPITALISM AND THE REFORMATION
THE THEORY OF CAPITALIST IMPERIALISM
ENLIGHTENED DESPOTISM

The Enlightenment

Jack Lively M A

FELLOW OF SAINT PETER'S COLLEGE
OXFORD

Enlightened 3. Possessed of mental light; instructed, well-informed; free from superstition or prejudice. 1663.

Enlightenment 2. Shallow and pretentious intellectualism, unreasonable contempt for authority and tradition, etc.; applied *esp.* to the spirit and aims of the French philosophers of the 18th c. 1865.

The Shorter Oxford English Dictionary

LONGMANS

LONGMANS GREEN AND CO LTD
48 Grosvenor Street, London WI

*Associated companies, branches and representatives
thoughout the world*

© Jack Lively 1966
First published 1966
Second impression 1967

*Printed in Great Britain by Richard Clay (The Chaucer Press), Ltd,
Bungay, Suffolk*

Editor's Foreword

'Study problems in preference to periods' was the excellent advice given by Lord Acton in his inaugural lecture at Cambridge. To accept it is one thing, to put it into practice is another. In fact, in both schools and universities the teaching of history, in depth, is often hindered by certain difficulties of a technical nature, chiefly to do with the availability of sources. In this respect, history tends to be badly off in comparison with literature or the sciences. The historical equivalents of set texts, readings or experiments, in which the student is encouraged to use his own mind, are the so-called 'special periods'. If these are to be fruitful, the student must be encouraged to deal in his own way with the problems raised by historical documents and the historiography of the issues in question and he must be made aware of the wider perspectives of history. Thus, if the enclosure movement of the sixteenth century is studied, the student might examine the historiographical explanations stretching from More's *Utopia* and Cobbett to Beresford's *Lost Villages of England*. At the same time he might also be dealing with selected documents raising important problems. Finally he might be encouraged to realize the problems of peasantries at other periods of time, including Russia and China in the nineteenth and twentieth centuries. In this particular instance, thanks to Tawney and Power, *Tudor Economic Documents*, the history teacher is comparatively well off. For other special periods the situation is much more difficult. If, however, the study of history is to encourage the development of the critical faculties as well as the memory, this approach offers the best hope. The object of this series is to go some way towards meeting these difficulties.

The general plan of volumes in the series will vary. Some historical problems lend themselves easily to a threefold division of historiography, documents and consideration of wider issues, but others do not. There has been no attempt to stretch authors upon the editorial rack and it will be noted that some volumes contain no documents. They will compensate for this by additional historiographical material.

A broad view is being taken of the limits of history. Political history will not be excluded, but a good deal of emphasis will be placed on economic, intellectual and social history. The idea has in fact grown out of the experience of a group of historians at the University of Sussex, where the student is encouraged to investigate the frontier areas between his own and related disciplines.

H. KEARNEY

Contents

VI *Optimism and the Problem of Evil*

VII *The Political Solution*

VIII *Progress and History*

Acknowledgements

We are indebted to the following for permission to reproduce copyright material:

Basil Blackwell & Mott Ltd for material from *L'Ancien Regime* by A. de Tocqueville, Tr. Patterson; the author for material from *The Age of Enlightenment* by Isaiah Berlin, published by Houghton Mifflin Company and The New American Library of World Literature, Inc. Copyright © 1956 by Isaiah Berlin; Cambridge University Press for material from *Political Tracts of Wordsworth, Coleridge and Shelley* edited by R. J. White, and *Natural Law and the Theory of Society* by O. Gierke; Jonathan Cape Ltd and George Braziller, Inc. for material from *In Search of Humanity* by Alfred Cobban; The Clarendon Press for material from *The Idea of History* by R. G. Collingwood; J. M. Dent & Sons Ltd and E. P. Dutton & Co. Inc. for material from *The Social Contract and Discourses* by Jean Jacques Rousseau, Tr. G. D. H. Cole (Everyman's Library 660); Dover Publications, Inc. New York for material from *Lectures on the Philosophy of History* by G. W. F. Hegel; the author for material from *The Faith of Reason* by Charles Frankel; the author, George Weidenfeld & Nicolson Ltd and Alfred A. Knopf, Inc. for 'Carl Becker's Heavenly City' and other extracts from *The Party of Humanity* by Peter Gay, Copyright © 1957 by Peter Gay: Copyright © 1959 by Princeton University Press; Hafner Publishing Company of New York for material from Newton's *Philosophy of Nature* edited by H. S. Thayer (Hafner Library of Classics); Harcourt, Brace World, Inc. for material from *English Thought in the Eighteenth Century*, Vol. I by Leslie Stephen, published by Rupert Hart-Davis Ltd; Harvard University Press for material from *The Great Chain of Being* by Arthur O. Lovejoy, and *Historical Pessimism in the French Enlightenment* by Henry Vyverberg, Copyright 1936 and 1958 respectively by the President and Fellows of Harvard College; Librairie A. Hatier for material from *European Thought in the Eighteenth Century* by Paul Hazard; The Johns Hopkins Press for material from *The Age of Crisis* by L. G. Crocker; The Macmillan Company for material from *The Works of Joseph de Maistre*, edited by Jack Lively; Thomas Nelson & Sons Ltd for material from *Dialogues Concerning Natural Religion* by David Hume, edited by Professor Norman Kemp Smith; Penguin Books Ltd for material from *Discourse on Method* by

R. Descartes, Tr. Arthur Wollaston (Penguin Classics 1960); Princeton University Press for material from *The Philosophy of the Enlightenment* by E. Cassirer, *Voltaire's Politics* by Peter Gay and *Diderot and Descartes* by A. Vartanian; Martin Secker & Warburg Ltd for material from *Origins of Totalitarian Democracy* by J. L. Talmon; Sheed & Ward Ltd for material from *The Image of Newton and Locke in the Age of Reason* by G. Buchdahl; the author for material from 'The Historical Philosophy of the Enlightenment' by Professor Hugh Kedward Trevor-Roper from *Studies on Voltaire and the Eighteenth Century*, Vol. 27 (1963), and Yale University Press for material from *The Heavenly City of the 18th Century Philosophers* by Carl Becker.

Introduction

Big historical concepts, like 'reformation' or 'capitalism' or 'imperialism', must always be in the historian's portfolio. Without them, he cannot hope to profit from his carefully gathered hoard of facts, will not indeed know which facts to gather. But those concepts only rarely belong to the past itself. Only occasionally is an age aware of itself or its ideas or its institutions as special and unique, differing radically from those of the past and preparing significantly for those of the future, worthy of a distinct historical label. Watershed, origin, rise, renaissance, crisis—all these are regularly in the historian's vocabulary. It is exceptional for an age, less socially introspective than our own, to express its own experience in such terms. The writers of the Enlightenment, acutely conscious of their distinctiveness and filled with a sense of their historical mission, were such an exception. Theirs was the age and they the men called to break with the traditions and authorities which had so long fettered mankind and to create through reason a new order of things.

Since they had so developed a sense of their election by fate, it might seem that our problems of definition should be easy. Whom are we to consider as within this movement? In what did its originality consist? What were its central ideas? Surely answers to these questions would be given clearly and unequivocally by such a self-conscious age. Yet in the event there is a great deal of disagreement amongst historians, even about the boundaries of the movement. For one, it stretches from Leibniz to Kant and finds its highest expression in Germany; for others it is fundamentally a French development, leaning heavily on Cartesian ideas; for yet another, it is largely the pursuit of the implications of British empirical philosophy. These views are all represented in Part Three of this book; but the assumption made in the selection of documents is that the movement was basically an intellectual dialogue between British and French thinkers.

How original was the Enlightenment? The answer really depends on the previous question. For if the Enlightenment is identified with the French *philosophes*, there is little in its philosophy that is strikingly new. They developed and even more popularized the ideas of the great seventeenth-century thinkers, but they did not question seriously their basic propositions. The sensationalism of Locke, the scientific empiricism of Bacon and Newton, the rationalism of Descartes, the optimism of Leibniz, the scepticism of Bayle, all were absorbed into their eclectic world view. Those thinkers who significantly dissented from this view —Hume, Berkeley, Vico—were either ignored or misunderstood by the *philosophes*. Yet their fusion of these older ideas gave birth to a radically new attitude towards knowledge and its application that justifies their own claim to have carried through a revolution in the human mind.

Fundamental to their belief in the unity and distinctiveness of their own ideas was the assumption that there is a body of truths, about man and society as well as about the world of nature, which can be rationally perceived, universally agreed and usefully applied to the welfare of mankind. Whatever the method of discovery, whether deduction from obvious fundamental truths or careful observation and generalization, sudden revelation or long accumulation of evidence, the mind alone or the mind and the senses, they did not doubt that these new techniques had been perfected for the exploration of previously unknown lands, whose new-found riches would transform the general quality of life.

These assumptions were deeply embedded in the *Encyclopédie*, the most solid monument and the aptest expression of the Enlightenment. Planned originally as a straightforward translation of Chambers's *Cyclopaedia*, it developed in the hands of Diderot and d'Alembert into a storehouse of Enlightenment wisdom. It typified the age, not only because its contributors included every great figure of the French Enlightenment (as well as many lesser writers) and because so many received opinions were expressed in it, but because the encyclopaedic form itself embodied the intellectual preconceptions and aspirations of the time. An encyclopaedia has a confident tone of voice. Here is a complete account of what is known, written by experts yet proposing what would be agreed by all reasonable men. Here is the language of statement and not of debate. Much of the *Encyclopédie* was devoted to what was known to the Victorians as 'useful knowledge', to technology and applied science; but the same note of certainty is sounded in the articles on pure science, metaphysics, morals and politics. An encyclopaedia also has an obvious aim, the diffusion of knowledge. In a learned journal, the expert speaks to the expert and, if the field is thought to be too large for this dialogue to take place, a rapid process of fission produces two learned journals. An encyclopaedia is dedicated to comprehending all knowledge and it presupposes both the possibility and the utility of the expert informing the layman. Thus the *Encyclopédie* reflected two aspects of the Enlightenment, two meanings of the word enlightenment. It rested on the belief that the age had discovered the means to certain knowledge; and it embodied the hope and expectation that light could be spread from the *philosophes* outwards. The advance of knowledge and the multiplication of the knowledgeable were its twin endeavours.

Besides these root assumptions, there were a number of philosophic positions very generally held. Descartes's rejection of tradition and authority as paths to truth was adopted without question. Allied to this was faith in the inherent rightness and the ultimate profitability of free inquiry into every subject. Restriction, censorship, persecution of beliefs were wrong, not only in that they added to the sum of human unhappiness, but because they blocked the achievement of their own aim, the establishment of truth. These claims inevitably brought Enlightenment thinkers into conflict with organized Christianity where, as in France (or, as Hume found, in Scotland), they were faced with a dogmatic and authoritarian church. But the sources of this hostility lay still deeper, in the expectation that everything in nature can be explained in empirical rather than spiritual terms. To understand the world is to know what its structure is and how it works, to discover its mechanism not its purposes, to describe rather than explain. Miracles and Providence were unsupported by any convincing evidence and, if true, would make impossible any coherent analysis of the empirical world; divine intervention in the universe, when it was allowed at all, was relegated to the first act of creation or impulsion. It is by observation and experiment above all that we can push forward our comprehension of the universe; what falls outside their scope is beyond knowledge. The nature of man and of the mind fall inside it, however; the human understanding and human nature can themselves be objects of scientific empirical inquiry. Such an investigation, it was thought, showed that all our ideas derive from the impressions we receive from the external world through our senses. It showed also that men's actions are determined by two primary motives, attraction to pleasure and aversion to pain. This hedonist psychology was translated into a hedonist ethic, the pursuit of happiness being taken as a standard for right action as well as a description of actual motivation: and through the utility principle, the principle of the greatest happiness of the greatest number, the hedonist ethic was converted into a ground for deciding governmental action. On the basis of this view that environment affected deeply men's understanding and nature, and on the belief that the means to reconstruct rationally the social system had been brought to light there grew a steady faith in the power of education and government to improve human life. There was a firm expectation, or at least a strong presumption, that, with the growth of knowledge and the increase in control over the environment, progress was assured.

Inevitably such a brief and summary sketch distorts a complex and sophisticated intellectual movement. It ignores the tensions within it, the variety of responses to common assumptions, the debates on questions of fundamental concern, the doubts and self-questioning of the *philosophes*, the development of ideas in time. Yet it is precisely because of this variety and development, these tensions, debates and doubts that difficulties of interpretation arise and historical controversy begins. To what extent did Descartes and Newton, did in other words *a priori* rationalism and empirical scientific thinking, respectively affect Enlightenment thought? How did epistemological theories influence social ideas? What were the religious positions of the *philosophes* and how fundamental was their antagonism to Christianity? How far did the secularization of thought extend and how confidently was it pursued? What solution was now offered to the problem of the existence of evil, so long explained in terms of the Christian dogma of original sin? Was eighteenth-century political thought liberal or totalitarian in its implications? What was the ancestry of the idea of progress and how deeply were Enlightenment thinkers committed to it? How true is the charge that they lacked any real historical insight? These are the questions which the documents here presented seek to illuminate and the historians here represented seek to answer.

Part One

SELECT DOCUMENTS

I

The Enlightenment's View of Itself

Perhaps the most general and striking feature of Enlightenment thought was its self-consciousness, its awareness of itself as a unique, distinctive and important moment in the development of the human mind. In the writings particularly of the French *philosophes*, there is reiterated a constantly expressed confidence in the new-found capacities of humanity and an equally constant desire to trace the genealogy of this liberation. Jean d'Alembert was amongst those most sensitive to the special role of his own age and conscious of the historical stages from which it had emerged. He was typical in that what he saw as peculiar to his own epoch was not a particular credo, not a particular set of beliefs, but a novel method of thought. Central to this method were systematic doubt of received opinions and rational analysis of the natural world, of social phenomena, of metaphysics, aesthetics, theology. These were the two sides of what the Enlightenment believed was its own special contribution to intellectual progress. That at least some *philosophes* saw its limitations is suggested by the dying fall at the end of the quotation.

1 D'Alembert's Sketch of the Human Mind in the Middle of the Eighteenth Century

Jean le Rond d'Alembert was born in in 1717, an illegitimate child abandoned near the church of S. Jean-le-Rond in Paris. Brought up by poor foster-parents, he showed his mathematical abilities at the Collège Mazarin. *It was as a mathematician, more particularly as the author of* Traité de dynamique, *that he came to prominence, but, as with most* philosophes, *his range of interests was extremely wide. He was co-editor with Diderot of the* Encyclopédie, *for which he wrote the* Discours préliminaire. *He died in 1783.*

From *Essai sur les élémens de philosophie.*

It seems that, for about three hundred years, nature has destined the middle of each century to be a period of revolution in the human mind. The capture of Constantinople in the middle of the fifteenth century brought about a renaissance in the literature of the West. The middle of the sixteenth century saw a rapid change in the religion and the disposition of a great part of Europe; the new dogmas of the reformers, upheld on the one side and attacked on the other with that fanaticism which God's work, well or badly understood, alone can inspire in men, forced both their defenders and their opponents to seek enlightenment; the rivalry stirred up by this great issue extended knowledge in every direction; and the light, kindled amidst error and discord, has shone on the very subjects which seem the furthest removed from these controversies. Finally Descartes, in the middle of the seventeenth century, founded a new philosophy, at first passionately attacked, then superstitiously espoused, and today reduced to its useful and true elements.

If one looks at all closely at the middle of our own century, the events that occupy us, our customs, our achievements and even our topics of conversation, it is difficult not to see that a very remarkable change in several respects has come in our ideas; a change which, by its rapidity, seems to us to foreshadow another still greater. Time alone will tell the aim, the nature and the limits of this revolution, whose inconveniences and advantages our posterity will recognize better than we can.

Every age that thinks well or badly, provided that it believes in thinking and thinks differently from the age which preceded it, takes on the title of *philosophic*; just as the title of *sages* is often accorded to those who have had no other talent than contradicting their contemporaries. Our age is thus called above all *the age of philosophy;* several writers have bestowed this name on it, persuaded that some glory is reflected on to them; others have refused it this honour, being incapable of sharing it.

If the present state of our knowledge is examined without bias, the progress of philosophy amongst us cannot be gainsaid. Natural science acquires new riches daily; geometry, pushing back its boundaries, has illuminated the parts of natural philosophy nearest to it; the true nature of the world has been discovered, developed and perfected; the same wisdom that had fixed the movements of celestial bodies has turned its attention to the bodies which surround us; by applying, or trying to apply geometry to the study of these bodies, it has been possible to perceive and determine the advantages and the misuses of this method; in a word, from the earth to Saturn, from the history of the heavens to that of insects, natural philosophy has changed its face. With it, almost all the other sciences have taken on a new shape, as indeed they must. A few reflections will convince us of this.

The study of nature seems in itself to be cold and untroubled, since the satisfaction it brings is a uniform, sustained and steady feeling and its pleasures, to be keen, must be intermittent and spasmodic. Nevertheless, the invention and the use of a new method of philosophy, the kind of enthusiasm that accompanies discoveries, a certain grandeur of ideas that the spectacle of the universe induces in us, all these causes have brought about a lively intellectual ferment. This ferment, active in every sense by its nature, has turned its attention with a sort of violence to everything that comes before it, like a river that has burst its banks. Now men seldom come back to a subject they have long neglected except to revise, for better or for worse, accepted ideas. The slower they are in shaking off the yoke of opinion, the more also, once they have broken its stranglehold on some points, they are ready to break it on all others; for they avoid even more the bother of investigation as they are not afraid of changing their minds; and as soon as they have once taken the trouble to retrace their steps, they regard and receive a new system of ideas as some sort of recompense for their courage and labour. Thus from the principles of the secular sciences to the foundations of revelation, from metaphysics to matters of taste, from music to morality, from the scholastic disputes of theologians to commercial subjects, from the rights of princes to those of peoples, from natural law to the arbitrary laws of nations, in a word from those questions which touch us most deeply to those which concern us least, everything has been discussed, analysed or at least brought into question. The fruit or the consequence of this general intellectual excitement has been to throw new light on some subjects and a new shadow on others, just as the effect of the ebb and flow of the sea is to cast some objects on the shore and to carry others away.

II

Rationalism

The systematic doubt placed by d'Alembert at the centre of Enlightenment thought was formulated as a method by René Descartes. In his philosophic method, Descartes rejected any reliance on authority and urged the acceptance only of what the mind could from its own resources know to be true. By this method, men could ascertain some fundamental truths. Since they are aware of themselves as subjects of thought, they can be sure of their own existence. The truth of this proposition can be known because we perceive it clearly and distinctly. Our clear and distinct (and thus our true) ideas are not gained from experience of the external world through the senses; nevertheless their truth can be assumed since we can be certain of the existence of a God whose essential nature would not allow him to deceive us. To prove the existence of God, Descartes uses the ontological proof, the argument that the existence of the idea of a perfect Being necessitates the existence of that perfect Being.

Cartesian thought was called into question by the end of the seventeenth century. In the field of natural science, his deductive rationalist approach was challenged by the inductive experimentalist view of Newton (see Section III). In epistemology, his theory of innate ideas (or what was taken to be his theory of innate ideas) was countered by Locke's sensationalist theory (see Section IV). In England and by the mid-eighteenth century in France, it was these rival positions that were dominant. Nevertheless, the question of the influence of Cartesian rationalism has remained a controversial one amongst Enlightenment scholars. A contemporary estimate of this influence, given by d'Alembert in his *Discours préliminaire* to the *Encyclopédie*, stresses the methodological inheritance of the Enlightenment from Cartesian philosophy.

2 Descartes's Systematic Doubt

René Descartes (1596-1650) had a profound effect upon the development of philosophy, mathematics and the natural sciences. He was educated by the Jesuits and spent some time in the army. In 1629, he left Paris for Holland and spent most of his productive intellectual life there. However, he did not thereby escape attacks from theologians and in 1648 he left Holland for Sweden, where he died two years later.

From *Discourse on Method*

In my early youth, I had made some study of logic in philosophy, and of geometry and algebra in mathematics, and it seemed that these three arts or sciences should contribute something to my design. But, when I examined them more closely, I saw that, as for logic, its syllogisms and most of its other modes of instruction rather serve to explain to others what one knows already, or even, as in the art of Lully,[1] to speak without judgment of what one does not know, than to acquire knowledge. And, although logic indeed contains many very true and excellent precepts, these are so confounded with so many others that are either harmful or superfluous that it is as difficult to distinguish the former as it would be to conjure up a statue of Diana or Minerva from an untouched block of marble. Then, with regard to the geometrical analysis of the ancients and the algebra of the moderns, besides the fact that both only deal with what is highly abstract and seems of no practical use, the former is so bound to the inspection of figures that it cannot exercise the understanding without greatly fatiguing the imagination, while the other is so subject to certain rules and a certain notation that it has become a confused and obscure art, which clogs the mind, rather than a science which cultivates its powers. That is why I thought I must look for some other method which would combine the advantages of these three disciplines, and yet be exempt from their defects. And, as a multiplicity of laws often provides excuses for vice, so that a State is much better governed when its few laws are very strictly observed, so, in place of the many precepts of which logic is composed, I thought I should have enough with the four following rules, provided I took a firm and constant resolution never once to fail to observe them.

The first rule was to accept as true nothing that I did not know to be

[1] The *Ars Magna* of Raymond Lully (1235–1315).

evidently so: that is to say, to avoid carefully precipitancy and prejudice, and to apply my judgments to nothing but that which showed itself so clearly and distinctly to my mind that I should never have occasion to doubt it.

The second was to divide each difficulty I should examine into as many parts as possible, and as would be required the better to solve it.

The third was to conduct my thoughts in an orderly fashion, starting with what was simplest and easiest to know, and rising little by little to the knowledge of the most complex, even supposing an order where there is no natural precedence among the objects of knowledge.

The last rule was to make so complete an enumeration of the links in an argument, and to pass them all so thoroughly under review, that I could be sure I had missed nothing.

3 Descartes's Metaphysical Certainty

From *Discourse on Method*

I had noticed long ago, as I have already pointed out, that, in matters of morality and custom, it is often necessary to follow opinions one knows to be highly doubtful, just as if there were no doubts attaching to them at all. Now, however, that I intended to make the search for truth my only business, I thought it necessary to do exactly the opposite, and to reject as absolutely false anything which gave rise in my mind to the slightest doubt, with the object of finding out, once this had been done, whether anything remained which I could take as indubitable. And so, because our senses sometimes deceive us, I made up my mind to suppose that they always did. Then, since there are men who fall into logical errors when they reason, even in the simplest geometrical matters, I reflected that I was as fallible as anyone, and rejected as false all the arguments I had hitherto regarded as conclusive. Finally, in view of the fact that those very same ideas, which come to us when we are awake, can also come when we are asleep without one of them then being true, I resolved to pretend that everything that had ever entered my mind was as false as the figments of my dreams. But then, immediately, as I strove to think of everything as false, I realized that, in the very act of thinking everything false, I was aware of myself as something real; and observing that the truth: *I think, therefore I am*, was so firm and so assured that the most extravagant arguments of the sceptics were incapable of shaking it, I concluded that I might have no scruple in taking it as that first principle of philosophy for which I was looking.

My next step was to examine attentively what I was, and here I saw that, although I could pretend that I had no body, and that there was neither world nor place in which I existed, I could by no means pretend that I myself was non-existent; on the contrary, from the mere fact that I could think of doubting the truth of other things, it followed quite clearly and evidently that I existed; whereas I should have had no reason to believe in my existence, had I but ceased to think for a moment, even if everything I had ever imagined had been true. I concluded that I was a substance whose whole essence or nature consists in thinking, and whose existence depends neither on its location in space nor on any material thing. Thus the self, or rather the soul, by which I am what I am, is entirely distinct from the body, is indeed easier to know than the body, and would not cease to be what it is, even if there were no body.

Next, I turned to a general consideration of what is required to ensure the truth and certitude of a proposition. I had just discovered one proposition of which I knew the truth to be assured, and I thought I should be able to learn in what this certitude consists. Observing that there is nothing in the proposition: *I think, therefore I am*, to assure me that I am speaking the truth, except that I see very clearly and distinctly that, in order to exist, one must think, I concluded that I could take as a general rule that the things we conceive very clearly and distinctly are all of them true, but that there is some difficulty in the proper discernment of distinct propositions.

Then, from reflecting on the fact that I had doubts, and that consequently my existence was not wholly perfect (for I saw clearly that it was a greater perfection to know than to doubt), it occurred to me to enquire how I had learned to think of something more perfect than myself, and it became evident to me that it must be through some nature which was in fact more perfect. As for the notions I had of many other things outside my mind, such as the sky, the earth, light, heat, and a thousand other things, I was not so much concerned to know whence these notions came to me, for I could see nothing in them that seemed to make them superior to me; if they were true, they came within the compass of my mind, in so far as my nature had any perfection, and if false, they arose out of nothing, inhabiting my mind only through some imperfection in my nature. But this could not be the case with the idea of a being more perfect than myself, for it was manifestly impossible that this idea should come to me from nothing; and I could not have acquired it of myself, since it is as repugnant to reason that the more perfect should proceed from the less perfect, and be dependent upon it, as it is that something should come out of nothing. I could only conclude that it had been placed in my mind by a nature really more perfect than mine, possessing indeed every perfection of which I could have any idea; that is to say, to express my meaning in a word, it had been placed in my mind by God. And I reflected further that I was not the only being that existed, for I knew that I lacked certain perfections, and that there must be, of necessity, some being more perfect than myself, on which I depended for my existence, and through which I had acquired every quality I possessed. For, if I had existed alone, in absolute independence of any other being, and possessing of myself the few qualities in which I participated through the perfect being, I might have had of myself, for the same reason, all those additional perfections I knew to be lacking in me. I could have been infinite, eternal, unmoved, all-knowing, and all powerful; I could have had all the perfections which I could see as existing in God. For, according to my reasoning so far, in order to know the nature of God in so far as my nature was capable of doing so, I had only to consider, with regard to each characteristic of which I had any idea, whether it were a measure of perfection, or not, to possess it; for I was sure that none of those that revealed any trace of imperfection was to be found in God, but that all the rest were. Thus I saw that doubt, inconsistency, melancholy, and so forth, were excluded from His nature, for I should have been glad to be exempt from them myself. There was also the fact that I had in my mind the ideas of many sensible and corporeal objects; I could suppose that I was dreaming, and that nothing I saw or imagined corresponded with the external reality, but I still could not deny that those ideas were really in my mind. But I had already seen clearly, by an examination of myself, that the intellectual nature is distinct from the corporeal, and so, considering that that which is composed of parts bears witness thereby to its contingent character, and that to be contingent is obviously an imperfection, I concluded that it could not be a mark of perfection in God to be composed of these two natures, and that consequently He was not so composed; and I also concluded that, if there were any bodies in the world, or any pure intelligences or any other beings which were not wholly perfect, their existence must depend on His power, in such a way that, without Him, they could not exist for a single moment.

4 The Influence of Descartes

From d'Alembert's *Discours préliminaire*

To Chancellor Bacon succeeded the illustrious Descartes. This rare man, whose reputation has so altered in less than a century, had all the qualities necessary to change the face of philosophy; a strong imagination, an extremely rational mind, knowledge drawn more from himself than from books, much courage in combating the most generally accepted prejudices, and no sort of dependence that might have forced him to compromise with them. He thus experienced in his own lifetime what commonly happens to everyone who gains too marked an ascendancy over others. He made some disciples and many enemies. Whether he understood his country or merely distrusted it, he took refuge in an entirely free land in order to meditate more easily. Although he thought much less of making disciples than meriting them, persecution sought him out in his retreat; and the cloistered life he led could not shield him from it. In spite of all the wisdom that he had employed in proving the existence of God, he was accused of denying it by officials who perhaps did not themselves believe it. Tormented and calumnied by foreigners and fairly badly received by his countrymen, he went to die in Sweden, doubtless far from anticipating the brilliant success that his opinions would one day have.

Descartes can be considered as a geometer or as a philosopher. Mathematics, on which he seems to have set very little value, nevertheless makes up today the most solid and least contested part of his renown. Algebra, created in some form by the Italians and prodigiously extended by our illustrious Viète, has been given new advancement in the hands of Descartes. One of the most important advances is his *method of indeterminates*, a most ingenious and subtle device which has since been applied to a great number of problems. But what has above all immortalized the name of this great man is his application of algebra to geometry, a more extensive and more fortunate idea than the human mind had ever previously had, and one which will always remain the key to the most profound research, not only in geometry but in all the physico-mathematical sciences.

As a philosopher, he has perhaps been as great but not as happy. Geometry, which by the nature of its subject matter must always gain without losing, could not but make very obvious progress, apparent to everyone, when in the hands of so great a genius. Philosophy was in a very different position, for in it nothing had been begun. How painful are the first steps in any field! The merit of making them excuses the fact that they are not greater. If Descartes, who has shown us the way, has not travelled as far along it as his followers believe, it is far from true that the sciences owe as little to him as his adversaries claim. His *method* alone would have been sufficient to make him immortal; his *Dioptrics* is the greatest and most satisfactory application of geometry to physical science that has yet been made; in fact, in his works, even those now least read, there can be seen throughout the flashes of an inventive genius. If his *vortices*, which have become almost ridiculous today, are judged without partiality, it will be agreed, I dare say, that nothing better could at that time have been imagined. The astronomical observations which have undermined them were still imperfect or patchy; nothing was more natural than to suppose a fluid that carried the planets; only a long series of phenomena, research and calculation, and consequently a long space of time, could overthrow so attractive a theory. It had moreover the special advantages of explaining the gravitation of bodies by the centrifugal force of the vortex itself: and I do not hesitate to say that this explanation of gravity is one of the most beautiful and ingenious hypotheses that philosophy has ever put forward. In consequence, in order to overthrow it, the physicists have had to involve themselves as if in spite of themselves in the theory of central forces and in experiments made a long time after. Let us then recognize that, forced to create an entirely new physical science, Descartes could not create a better one, that it was necessary, so to speak, to pass through the vortices in order to reach a true theory of the world, and that, if he was mistaken about the laws of movement, at least he was the first to predict that there had to be such laws.

His metaphysics, as ingenious and as novel as his physics, has had very nearly the same fate; and also very nearly the same reasons can justify it. For such is today the reputation of this great man that, having had disciples without number, he is almost reduced to apologists. He was no doubt mistaken in accepting innate ideas: but if he had retained from the Peripatetic sect the only truth that it taught on the origin of ideas in the senses, perhaps the errors which dishonoured this truth by their association with it would have been more difficult to uproot. Descartes at least dared to show advanced minds how to shake off the yoke of scholasticism, of opinion, of authority, in a word of prejudices and barbarism. By this revolt, whose fruits we today gather, he rendered to philosophy a service more essential perhaps than all those it owes to his well-known successors. He can be regarded as a rebel leader who has had the courage to rise up first against a despotic and arbitrary power, and who, in preparing a glorious revolution, has laid the foundations for a government more just and more felicitous than any he could imagine. If he finished by believing everything explained, at least he started by doubting everything; and the arms we use to attack him belong to him no less because we turn them against him. Moreover, when absurd opinions are deep-rooted, it is sometimes necessary, in order to disabuse humanity, to replace them by other errors, when nothing better can be done. The uncertainty and the vanity of the mind is such that it always needs an opinion on which it can fasten. It is a child to whom a toy must be given in order to remove a dangerous weapon from it; it will of itself leave aside this toy when the age of reason has arrived. By having to make this exchange, philosophers, or at least those who think themselves such, are at least taught to distrust their own understanding, and this frame of mind is the first step towards the truth. So Descartes was persecuted in his lifetime as if he had brought it to men.

III

Empiricism

The influence of Sir Isaac Newton on the progress of both the natural and the social sciences was far reaching. Whilst this is generally agreed, there is considerable disagreement on the nature of his influence. For Cassirer, it is Newton's methodology, his insistence that hypotheses must be based solely on experience of the empirical world, that dominated the Enlightenment and gave it its distinctive tone (see pp. 126–31). Buchdahl distinguishes two different and to some degree contradictory effects of Newton's achievement; one was the importance attached to observation and the experimental method, but another was the admiration showered on the vast synthesizing scientific theory as exemplified in Newton's laws of motion and gravitation (see pp. 131–4). Vartanian also distinguishes these two aspects of eighteenth-century scientific endeavour, but traces the second to Descartes rather than Newton.

The two extracts from Newton illustrate these two sides of his thought, whilst the quotation from Buffon points to both the caution and the ambition of the scientific method. Condillac, in his *Traité des systèmes*, conducted the most thorough attack on seventeenth-century metaphysicians and their *esprit de système*, posing as the proper alternative the *esprit systématique*, the analytic method based on developing explanatory concepts from empirical knowledge. Not all thinkers were as enthusiastic about the Newtonian method. Fontenelle, who remained faithful to Cartesian physics, compared Newton to Descartes in a way which, according to Voltaire's report, offended Newton's English disciples.

The experimental method was not thought of just as a means of exploring the natural world. One of the Enlightenment's most persistent concerns was to construct scientific explanations of man and society. The extracts from Hume and Montesquieu stress that social and psychological as well as physical knowledge must rest on experiment and observation.

5 Newton and the Experimental Method

Sir Isaac Newton (1642-1727) was born in Lincolnshire and educated at Trinity College, Cambridge. He became a fellow of his college in 1667 and remained in Cambridge until he left to take up a post in the Mint in 1696. His principal works were the Optics *and the* Principia, *in which he expounded his theory of gravitation. His reputation in the eighteenth century was immense, as much because he was thought to exemplify perfectly the scientific method as because of the importance of his particular discoveries.*

From a letter to Oldenburg

... For the best and safest method of philosophizing seems to be, first, to inquire diligently into the properties of things and to establish those properties by experiments, and to proceed later to hypotheses for the explanation of things themselves. For hypotheses ought to be applied only in the explanation of the properties of things, and not made use of in determining them; except in so far as they may furnish experiments. And if anyone offers conjectures about the truth of things from the mere possibility of hypotheses, I do not see by what stipulation anything certain can be determined in any science; since one or another set of hypotheses may always be devised which will appear to supply new difficulties. Hence I judged that one should abstain from contemplating hypotheses, as from improper argumentation. ...

6 Newton's Philosophy of Nature

From the Preface to the *Principia*

I offer this work as the mathematical principles of philosophy, for the whole burden of philosophy seems to consist in this: from the phenomena of motions to investigate the forces of nature, and then from these forces to demonstrate the other phenomena; and to this end the general propositions in the First and Second Books are directed. In the Third Book I give an example of this in the explication of the System of the World; for by the propositions mathematically demonstrated in the former books, in the third I derive from the celestial phenomena the forces of gravity with which bodies tend to the sun and the several planets. Then from these forces, by other propositions which are also mathematical, I deduce the motions of the planets, the comets, the moon, and the sea. I wish we could derive the rest of the phenomena of Nature by the same kind of reasoning from mechanical principles, for I am induced by many reasons to suspect that they may all depend upon certain forces by which the particles of bodies, by some causes hitherto unknown, are either mutually impelled toward one another and cohere in regular figures, or are repelled and recede from one another. These forces being unknown, philosophers have hitherto attempted the search of Nature in vain; but I hope the principles here laid down will afford some light either to this or some truer method of philosophy.

7 Buffon on the Methods and Aims of Natural Science

Georges Louis Leclerc de Buffon (1707–88) was a naturalist who won a high reputation in his own day. He was appointed as a young man to the director-ship of the Jardin du Roi, *and there between 1749 and 1767 he produced the fifteen volumes of his* Histoire naturelle.

From *De la manière d'étudier l'histoire naturelle*

One must start by observing much and re-observing often: however necessary close attention is, here it can be avoided at first—I am speaking of that scrupulous care which is always useful when much is known, but is often harmful to those who are just starting to improve their minds. The essential thing is to furnish their minds with ideas and facts, and, if at all possible, to prevent them drawing arguments and connections from them too soon; for it always happens that, through ignorance of certain facts and through too few ideas, they exhaust their minds with false theories and burden their memories with vague inferences and conclusions contrary to the truth, which subsequently breed prejudices difficult to extirpate.

This is why I said that it is necessary to start by observing much; it is also necessary to observe almost without purpose, for once you have decided to look at things only from a certain point of view, in a certain order, within a certain system, even if you have chosen the best course, you will never achieve the same extent of knowledge as if you started by allowing your mind to wander freely, to find its own bearings, to fix itself unaided and to construct alone the primary chain which represents the order of its ideas. . . .

I have been struck . . . by a fault or an excess that is found throughout almost all the books written a century or two ago, and that German scholars still have today; this is the amount of useless erudition with which they deliberately swell their works, so that the subject they are dealing with is swamped under a mass of extraneous material about which they argue with so much self-satisfaction and spread themselves with so little regard for their readers that they seem to have forgotten what they have to tell you in order to recount to you what others have said. I imagine a man like Aldrovande, having once conceived the aim of writing a comprehensive encyclopaedia of natural history; I see him in his library reading successively the ancients, moderns, philosophers, theologians, jurists, historians, travellers, poets, and reading with no other purpose than to grasp from near and from far all the words and phrases that bear on his subject; I see him copying and having copied all these remarks and arranged them in alphabetical order, having filled several portfolios with notes of this kind, often taken hastily and indiscriminately, he starts to work on a particular subject, not wishing to lose anything of what he has gathered together; so that when he comes to the natural history of the cock or the bull, he tells you everything that has ever been said about cocks or bulls, everything the ancients thought about them, everything that has been conceived of their virtues, their character, their courage, all the uses to which they have been put, all the old wives' tales about them, all the miracles that they have been made to perform in certain religions, all the subjects of superstition that they have supplied, all the similes poets have drawn from them, all the attributes that certain peoples have given to them, all the representations of them in hieroglyphics and in heraldry, in a word all the stories and all the fables that have ever come into men's heads on the subject of cocks or bulls. After this, you can estimate the amount of natural history that you can expect to find in this hotch-potch of quotations; and indeed if the author has not put it in some articles separated from the others, it will not be there to be found, or at least it will not be worth the trouble of seeking it out.

This fault has been completely corrected in this age; the order and precision of writing nowadays have made the sciences easier and more attractive, and I am convinced that this difference of style contributes perhaps as much to their advancement as the spirit of research which is today supreme; for our predecessors investigated like us, but they gathered together everything that presented itself, whilst we reject what seems to us of little value and prefer a well-argued small work to an erudite massive volume; the only danger is that, distrusting erudition, we will also come to imagine that the mind can make up for everything and that science is only a vain name.

However, sensible people will always feel that the only true science is the knowledge of facts, the mind cannot be a substitute for it and facts are in the sciences what experience is in civil life. . . .

I have said that the faithful history and the exact description of each thing are the two sole objects that should be pursued at first in the study of natural history. The ancients amply achieved the first, and are perhaps as far beyond the moderns in this first aspect, as the latter are beyond them in the second. . . .

Nevertheless [the explanation of natural phenomena] is the most important objective, and it should not be imagined, even today, that in the study of natural history we should limit ourselves solely to giving exact descriptions and making sure of particular facts; this is in truth, and as I have said, the essential end we should set ourselves at first, but we must try to rise to something greater and more worthy of occupying us; this is, to arrange our observations, to generalise our facts, to link them together by means of analogies, and to try to reach that high level of knowledge where we can judge that particular processes depend upon more general processes, where we can compare nature with itself in its great operations, and from which we can observe the ways to perfect the different parts of physical science. A good memory, application and attention are sufficient to reach the first end; but the second needs something more, it needs general views, a firm understanding and an intellect formed more by reflection than by study; finally it needs that quality of mind which enables us to grasp the most distant connections, to gather them together and to form from them a body of reasoned ideas, after having determined exactly their likelihood and having weighed their probability.

8 Condillac and *l'Esprit de Système*

Étienne Bonnot de Condillac (1715–80) was born into a noble family and took a familiar route into the priesthood, in which he remained despite his material-ist beliefs. He was amongst the most vigorous exponents in France of sen-sationalist philosophy.

From *Traité des systèmes*

A system is nothing other than the arrangement of the different parts of an art or a science in an order in which they all give each other mutual support, and in which the last are explained by the first. Those which explain others are called *principles;* and the system is the more perfect the fewer are the principles. It is even to be hoped that they can be reduced to a single one.

Three sorts of principles can be distinguished in philosophic works, from which three sorts of systems are derived.

The principles that I put in the first category, as the most in vogue, are general or abstract maxims. It is claimed that they are so evident, or so well demonstrated, that they cannot be called into question. Indeed, if they were uncertain, no sure consequences could be drawn from them.

These are the sort of principles about which the author of *L'art de penser*[1] speaks when he says: 'Everyone is agreed that it is important to hold in the mind several axioms and principles which, being clear and indisputable, can serve us as a basis for understanding the most obscure subjects. But those that are ordinarily offered are of so little use, that it is futile to know them. For what is called the first principle of know-ledge, *that it is impossible for the same thing both to be and not to be*, is certainly clear and certain; but I see no possible occasion on which it could help us to acquire knowledge. I therefore believe that these could be more useful.'

He then gives as a first principle, that *everything which is included in the clear and distinct idea of a thing can be affirmed of it with truth:* for a second, that *its at least possible existence is included in the idea of each thing that we conceive clearly and distinctly;* for a third, that *nothingness cannot give rise to anything*. He has thought up as many as eleven of these. But it is use-less to quote the others; these will suffice as an example.

[1] Arnauld and Nicole in *La logique ou l'art de penser.*

The virtue that philosophers attribute to this kind of principle is so great that it is natural for men to work to multiply them. Metaphysicians have distinguished themselves in this. Descartes, Malebranche, Leibniz, etc., each has vied in lavishing them on us, and we have only ourselves to blame if we do not penetrate *the most obscure subjects*.

A second category of principles are hypotheses invented to explain things that cannot be otherwise explained.[1] If these hypotheses do not seem impossible, and if they provide some explanation of known phenomena, the philosophers have no doubt that they have laid bare the true springs of nature. Would it be possible, they say, for an hypothesis which was false to provide such happy solutions.

From this arises the view that the explanation of phenomena proves the truth of an hypothesis, and that a system should be judged not so much by its principles as by the way in which it accounts for things. On this view, the hypotheses, at first arbitrary, become beyond dispute incontestable by the skill with which they have been used.

The metaphysicians have been as prolific in this second kind of principle as in the first; and, through their labours, there is no longer any subject that can be a mystery for metaphysics. Who speaks metaphysics speaks, in their language, the science of primary truths, of the first principles of things. But it must be admitted that this science is not to be found in their works.

Abstract ideas are only ideas formed from the common elements of several particular ideas. Such is the concept of animal: it is the common denominator of the ideas of man, horse, monkey, etc. Through this an abstract idea apparently serves to give an explanation of what is observed in particular objects. For example, if one asks why a horse walks, drinks or eats, the very philosophic reply will be given, simply because it is an animal. However, this reply, properly analysed, means nothing save that the horse walks, drinks, eats because in fact it walks, drinks, eats. But it is rare for men not to be content with the first reply. It might be said that their curiosity leads them less to instruct themselves on one subject than to pose questions on several. The confident air of the philosopher deceives them. They fear to appear too stupid if they insist on the same point. It is enough that the given pronouncement is made up of familiar expressions for them to be ashamed not to understand it; or if they cannot blink its obscurity, a single glance from their master appears to dissipate it. Can one doubt when he to whom one has confided all one's trust does not himself doubt? It is not therefore

[1] Descartes, *Principes*, Book III, para. 44.

surprising that abstract principles have multiplied so greatly, and have at all times been regarded as the source of our knowledge.

Abstract concepts are absolutely necessary to set our knowledge in order, since they give its classification to each idea. This is the only way in which they should be used. But to imagine that they are made to lead to particular knowledge is a blindness all the greater as they are formed only after this knowledge. When I condemn abstract principles, I should not therefore be suspected of demanding that no use should any longer be made of any abstract idea; this would be ridiculous. I claim only that they should never be taken as appropriate principles to lead to discoveries.

As for hypotheses, they are such an aid and so comforting to ignorance; imagination makes them with so much pleasure, with so little pain; it is in their grip that one creates, that one governs the universe. All this costs no more than a dream, and a philosopher dreams easily.

It is not so easy to consult experience properly and to gather facts discriminatingly. This is why it is rare for us to take as principles only well-established facts, although perhaps we have many more of them than we think; but, through making little use of them, we do not know how to apply them. We have really in our hands the explanation of a number of phenomena, but we seek it very much further off. For instance, the gravity of bodies has always been a well-established fact, yet it is only in our own day that it has been recognized as a principle.

It is on principles of this last kind that are founded true systems, those that alone merit the name. For it is only by means of these principles that we can explain those things whose workings we are permitted to discover.

9 Newton and Descartes

Bernard le Bovyer de Fontenelle (1657–1757), typifying the versatility of his age, attempted nearly every form of literature and threw himself into every kind of controversy. In the quarrel between the Ancients and the Moderns, he sided with the Moderns; in his Histoire des oracles, *he covertly attacked Christianity; in the* Entretiens sur la pluralité des mondes, *he popularized Copernican astronomy. In this last work he retained the vortices of Cartesian physics. He remained faithful to Descartes despite the growing influence of Newton in France.*

From Fontenelle's *Eloge de Newton* to the Académie des Sciences (1727)

[Descartes and Newton], who stand in such direct opposition, have had much in common. Both were geniuses of the first order, born to dominate other minds and to establish empires. Both were excellent geometers and saw the need for applying geometry to physics. Both founded their physics on a geometry that they derived almost wholly from their own understanding. But the one, setting off on an audacious flight, wanted to find the source of all things and to make himself master of first principles through some clear and fundamental ideas, in order that henceforward he should only descend to natural phenomena as necessary consequences. The other, more timid or more modest, started his journey by relying on phenomena in order to climb up to unknown principles, resolved to admit them whatever the logical sequence that gave them. The one starts from what he understands clearly to find the cause of what he sees. The other starts from what he sees to find its cause, whether it be clear or obscure. The evident principles of the one do not always lead to phenomena as they are. The phenomena do not always lead the other to such evident principles. The limits which, along these two opposite paths, have halted two men of this kind are not limits of their minds but those of the human intelligence.

François Marie Arouet de Voltaire (1694–1778) stands at the head of Enlightenment writers. Although not the most original thinker of his age, he was the most prolific and far-ranging. Philosophy, poetry, drama, novels, history, political polemics and scientific works flowed from his pen. Although he was no stranger to royal courts, his writings inevitably attracted persecution by the authorities, and he suffered both imprisonment and exile. During one early period of banishment to England, between 1726 and 1729, he mastered the elements of Newton's astronomical physics.

From Voltaire's letter 'On Descartes and Newton' in *Lettres philosophiques*

This famous Newton, this destroyer of the Cartesian system, died in March of last year, 1727. He lived honoured by his fellow-countrymen, and was buried like a king who had guarded the welfare of his subjects.

The eulogy on Mr Newton delivered by M. de Fontenelle to the

Académie des Sciences has been read eagerly here and has been translated into English. The opinion of M. de Fontenelle was awaited in England as a solemn declaration of the superiority of English philosophy; but when it was seen that he compared Descartes to Newton, the whole of the Royal Society of London rose up in revolt. Far from agreeing with this opinion, this discourse has been criticized; several (and these are not the most philosophic) have even been shocked by this comparison simply because Descartes was French. . . .

I do not believe that [Descartes's] philosophy can in truth be compared in any way with that of Newton; the first is an essay, the second is a masterpiece; but he who has set us on the road to truth is perhaps of more value than he who has since travelled the whole of this road.

10 The Science of Man

David Hume (1711–76) was born in Edinburgh, a city in which he spent much of his life. After dabbling in law and business he left for France in 1734, and there wrote his Treatise of Human Nature, *which went unnoticed on its publication in 1739. The fame that eluded him as a philosopher came to him as an essayist and historian. In 1763 he was appointed as secretary to the British Embassy in Paris and there met most of the leading figures of the French Enlightenment. Although they welcomed him as a fellow philosopher, most did not realize the full revolutionary implications of his thought. The* Dialogues Concerning Natural Religion *was not published until after his death though written much earlier.*

From Hume's *Treatise of Human Nature*

And, as the science of man is the only solid foundation for the other sciences, so, the only solid foundation we can give to this science itself must be laid on experience and observation. It is no astonishing reflection to consider, that the application of experimental philosophy to moral subjects should come after that to natural, at the distance of above a whole century; since we find in fact, that there was about the same interval betwixt the origins of these sciences; and that, reckoning from Thales to Socrates, the space of time is nearly equal to that betwixt my Lord Bacon and some late philosophers[1] in England, who

[1] Mr Locke, my Lord Shaftesbury, Dr Mandeville, Mr Hutchinson, Dr Butler, etc.

have begun to put the science of man on a new footing, and have engaged the attention, and excited the curiosity of the public. So true it is, that however other nations may rival us in poetry, and excel us in some other agreeable arts, the improvements in reason and philosophy can only be owing to a land of toleration and of liberty.

Nor ought we to think, that this latter improvement in the science of man will do less honour to our native country than the former in natural philosophy, but ought rather to esteem it a greater glory, upon account of the greater importance of that science, as well as the necessity it lay under of such a reformation. For to me it seems evident, that the essence of the mind being equally unknown to us with that of external bodies, it must be equally impossible to form any notion of its powers and qualities otherwise than from careful and exact experiments, and the observation of those particular effects, which result from its different circumstances and situations. And though we must endeavour to render all our principles as universal as possible, by tracing up our experiments to the utmost, and explaining all effects from the simplest and fewest causes, it is still certain we cannot go beyond experience; and any hypothesis, that pretends to discover the ultimate original qualities of human nature, ought at first to be rejected as presumptuous and chimerical.

Charles de Secondat, baron de Montesquieu (1689–1755) was president of the parlement *of Bordeaux from 1716 until he retired in 1726 and moved to Paris to devote himself to writing. Whilst in Bordeaux, he had published his satire on French society, the* Lettres persanes. *After his move to Paris, he spent a good deal of time in travel, studying the political and social institutions of European states. The fruits of this study came with the publication of* De l'esprit des lois *in 1748.*

From the preface to De l'esprit des lois

I have first of all considered mankind, and the result of my thoughts has been, that amidst such an infinite diversity of laws and manners, they were not solely conducted by the caprice of fancy.

I have laid down the first principles, and have found that the particular cases follow naturally from them; that the histories of all nations are only consequences of them; and that every particular law is connected with another law, or depends on some other of a more general extent.

When I have been obliged to look back into antiquity I have endeavoured to assume the spirit of the ancients, lest I should consider those things as alike which are really different, and lest I should miss the difference of those which appear to be alike.

I have not drawn my principles from my prejudices, but from the nature of things.

Here a great many truths will not appear till we have seen the chain which connects them with others. The more we enter into particulars, the more we shall perceive the certainty of the principles on which they are founded.

IV

Epistemology and Psychology

It seemed natural to extend the scientific method to problems of man and society. The investigation of the human mind had to be conducted on the same principles as the investigation of nature, on observation and experiment, and the nature of knowledge to be explained in terms of the physiology of the mind. But the scientific explanation of the mind and the discovery of factually based truths about its working was more than just an extension to another area of inquiry of a method successful in illuminating the natural world; it was the necessary foundation of any knowledge. Before men could be sure of the results of their investigations, into the natural world, into religion, into morals or politics, they must be certain of the adequacy of their tools. Before they could know anything, they must know how they know. This is the justification given by Locke and Hume for their inquiries into the human understanding and human nature, and this is the reason why epistemology assumed a central role in Enlightenment thought.

The explanation of the nature of knowledge most commonly accepted was that given by Locke (see pp. 30–32). Starting with an attack upon innate ideas, Locke went on to base the whole of knowledge on the sensations and reflection. The mind is a *tabula rasa* on which experience, either of the external world or of its own operations, imprints ideas. The basic and irreducible components of thought, the simple ideas, are reflections of the outside world perceived by the mind through the senses, and complex ideas are built up by piecing together these basic components. This theory created difficulties discerned by some philosophers. Berkeley saw that, if men can only know sense experiences, then they can have no assurance of the reality of the material world to which the mind relates those experiences. Hume, distinguishing between formal mathematical reasoning and statements about the external world, argued that our knowledge of casual relations between phenomena in the real world cannot be certain but are merely inferences drawn from the habitual conjunction of different events. Nevertheless, most *philosophes* were willing to swallow Locke's theory whole. D'Alembert, in the *Preliminary Discourse*, echoed him faithfully and dismissed impatiently the kind of objection Berkeley put to sensationalism (see pp. 32–35). Condillac gave one of the most celebrated accounts of the theory in his *Traité des sensations*, in which he used the analogy of a statue wakened to life and understanding through its gradual acquisition of the senses. Nevertheless, Condillac criticized Locke for allowing innate ideas back into his theory in the guise of reflection (see p. 35). Condillac could dispense with the notion of reflection or subsume it under sensation through his theory of language. Through language man can recall past sensations and is not therefore subject to the chances of passing experience. By language he can recover at will the ideas attached to words by previous sensation and so can organize his thought independently of his immediate confrontation with the external world. The technique of language creates the possibility of reflection, but reflection none the less rests on sensation. The final materialist conclusion to which sensationalism was pushed is illustrated by the extract from La Mettrie (see pp. 35–36). For the materialist, neither the universe nor man had a spiritual element, both being governed completely and exclusively by laws of matter.

As the quotation from the *Preliminary Discourse* shows, this epistemology was closely associated with a psychological theory which saw men as being motivated by the pursuit of pleasure and the avoidance of pain. D'Holbach, in his *System of Nature*, exemplifies the transformation of this theory into a particular notion of both the origins of moral feelings and the nature of virtue and vice (see pp. 37–38). On this view, the concept of good and bad action has arisen through man's appreciation that the actions of others affect his happiness and that his actions affect the happiness of others; and the objective standard of good and bad action is in fact the degree to which an action promotes pleasure or causes pain.

The general effect of this complex of ideas was to emphasize the role of environment and education in the shaping of ideas and attitudes. With the discrediting of traditional Christian explanations of the existence of evil and the attack upon the fashionable Leibnizian optimism, this emphasis assumed a powerful revolutionary potential.

11 The Foundations of Knowledge

*John Locke (1632–1704) formulated the conventional wisdom of the Enlighten-
ment, laying the foundations for both its theory of knowledge and its political
ideas. He was born in Somerset, the son of an attorney, and was educated at
Oxford, where he remained for a time as a tutor. He came under the patronage
of the first Earl of Shaftesbury and shared his political fortunes, being exiled
with him in 1683 and returning to England only after the Glorious Revolution.* A Letter Concerning Toleration *appeared in 1689 and his two most
important works, the* Essay Concerning Human Understanding *and the*
Two Treatises of Government, *followed in 1690.*

From Locke's *Essay Concerning Human Understanding*

I thought that the first step towards satisfying several inquiries the
mind of man was very apt to run into, was, to take a survey of our own
understandings, examine our own powers, and see to what things they
were adapted. Till that was done I suspected we began at the wrong
end, and in vain sought for satisfaction in a quiet and sure possession of
truths that most concerned us, whilst we let loose our thoughts into the
vast ocean of Being; as if all that boundless extent were the natural and
undoubted possession of our understandings, wherein there was nothing
exempt from its decisions, or that escaped its comprehension. Thus
men, extending their inquiries beyond their capacities, and letting their
thoughts wander into those depths where they can find no sure footing,
it is no wonder that they raise questions and multiply disputes, which,
never coming to any clear resolution, are proper only to continue and
increase their doubts, and to confirm them at last in perfect scepticism.
Whereas, were the capacities of our understandings well considered,
the extent of our knowledge once discovered, and the horizon found
which sets the bounds between the enlightened and dark parts of
things—between what is and what is not comprehensible by us—men
would perhaps with less scruple acquiesce in the avowed ignorance of
the one, and employ their thoughts and discourse with more advantage
and satisfaction in the other.

From Hume's *Treatise of Human Nature*

It is evident, that all the sciences have a relation, greater or less, to human nature; and that, however wide any of them may seem to run from it, they still return back by one passage or another. Even *Mathematics*, *Natural Philosophy*, and *Natural Religion*, are in some measure dependent on the science of MAN; since they lie under the cognisance of men, and are judged of by their powers and faculties. It is impossible to tell what changes and improvements we might make in these sciences were we thoroughly acquainted with the extent and force of human understanding, and could explain the nature of the ideas we employ, and of the operations we perform in our reasonings. And these improvements are the more to be hoped for in natural religion, as it is not content with instructing us in the nature of superior powers, but carries its views further, to their disposition towards us, and our duties towards them; and consequently, we ourselves are not only the beings that reason, but also one of the objects concerning which we reason.

If, therefore, the sciences of mathematics, natural philosophy, and natural religion, have such a dependence on the knowledge of man, what may be expected in the other sciences, whose connection with human nature is more close and intimate? The sole end of logic is to explain the principles and operations of our reasoning faculty, and the nature of our ideas; morals and criticism regard our tastes and sentiments; and politics consider men as united in society, and dependent on each other. In these four sciences of *Logic*, *Morals*, *Criticism* and *Politics*, is comprehended almost everything which it can anyway import us to be acquainted with, or which can tend either to the improvement or ornament of the human mind.

Here then is the only expedient, from which we can hope for success in our philosophical researches, to leave the tedious lingering method, which we have hitherto followed, and, instead of taking now and then a castle or village on the frontier, to march up directly to the capital or centre of these sciences, to human nature itself; which being once masters of, we may everywhere else hope for an easy victory. From this station we may extend our conquests over all those sciences, which more intimately concern human life, and may afterwards proceed at leisure, to discover more fully those which are the objects of pure curiosity. There is no question of importance, whose decision is not comprised in the science of man; and there is none, which can be decided with any certainty, before we become acquainted with that science. In pretending, therefore, to explain the principles of human nature, we in effect propose a complete system of the sciences, built on a foundation almost entirely new, and the only one upon which they can stand with any security.

12   The Origins of Ideas

From Locke's *Essay Concerning Human Understanding*

It is an established opinion amongst some men, that there are in the understanding certain *innate principles*; some primary notions, κοιναὶ ἔννοιαι, characters, as it were stamped upon the mind of man; which the soul receives in its very first being, and brings into the world with it. It would be sufficient to convince unprejudiced readers of the falseness of this supposition, if I should only show (as I hope I shall in the following parts of this Discourse) how men, barely by the use of their natural faculties, may attain to all the knowledge they have, without the help of any innate impressions; and may arrive at certainty, without any such original notions or principles. For I imagine anyone will easily grant that it would be impertinent to suppose the ideas of colours innate in a creature to whom God hath given sight, and a power to receive them by the eyes from external objects: and no less unreasonable would it be to attribute several truths to the impressions of nature, and innate characters, when we may observe in ourselves faculties fit to attain as easy and certain knowledge of them as if they were originally imprinted on the mind.

.   .   .

Every man being conscious to himself that he thinks; and that which his mind is applied about whilst thinking being the *ideas* that are there, it is past doubt that men have in their minds several ideas—such as are those expressed by the words *whiteness, hardness, sweetness, thinking, motion, man, elephant, army, drunkenness*, and others: it is in the first place then to be inquired how he comes by them.

Let us then suppose the mind to be, as we say, white paper void of all characters, without any ideas. How comes it to be furnished? Whence comes it by that vast store which the busy and boundless fancy of man has painted on it with an almost endless variety? Whence has it all the *materials* of reason and knowledge? To this I answer, in one word, from

EXPERIENCE. In that all our knowledge is founded; and from that it ultimately derives itself. Our observation, employed either about *external sensible objects, or about the internal operations of our minds perceived and reflected on by ourselves, is that which supplies our understandings with all the materials of thinking*. These two are the fountains of knowledge, from whence all the ideas we have, or can naturally have, do spring.

First, our Senses, conversant about particular sensible objects, do convey into the mind several distinct perceptions of things, according to those various ways wherein those objects do affect them. And thus we come by those *ideas* we have of *yellow, white, heat, cold, soft, hard, bitter, sweet*, and all those which we call sensible qualities; which when I say the senses convey into the mind, I mean, they from external objects convey into the mind what produces there those perceptions. This great source of most of the ideas we have, depending wholly upon our senses, and derived by them to the understanding, I call SENSATION.

Secondly, the other fountain from which experience furnisheth the understanding with ideas is the perception of the operations of our own mind within us, as it is employed about the ideas it has got; which operations, when the soul comes to reflect on and consider, do furnish the understanding with another set of ideas, which could not be had from things without. And such are *perception, thinking, doubting, believing, reasoning, knowing, willing*, and all the different actings of our own minds; which we being conscious of, and observing in ourselves, do from these receive into our understandings as distinct ideas as we do from bodies affecting our senses. This source of ideas every man has wholly in himself; and though it be not sense, as having nothing to do with external objects, yet it is very like it, and might properly enough be called *internal sense*. But as I call the other Sensation, so I call this REFLECTION, the ideas it affords being such only as the mind gets by reflecting on its own operations within itself. By reflection then, in the following part of this discourse, I would be understood to mean, that notice which the mind takes of its own operations, and the manner of them, by reason whereof there come to be ideas of these operations in the understanding. These two, I say, viz. external material things, as the objects of SENSATION, and the operations of our own minds within, as the objects of REFLECTION, are to me the only originals from whence all our ideas take their beginnings. The term *operations* here I use in a large sense, as comprehending not barely the actions of the mind about its ideas, but some sort of passions arising sometimes from them, such as is the satisfaction or uneasiness arising from any thought.

The understanding seems to me not to have the least glimmering of any ideas which it doth not receive from one of these two. *External objects* furnish the mind with the ideas of sensible qualities, which are all those different perceptions they produce in us; and *the mind* furnishes the understanding with ideas of its own operations.

From D'Alembert's *Discours préliminaire*

All our knowledge can be divided into direct and reflective knowledge. Direct knowledge is that which we receive immediately without any intervention of our will. This knowledge, finding all the doors of our soul open, so to speak, enters unhindered and effortlessly. Reflective knowledge is that which the mind acquires by operating on, unifying and combining direct knowledge.

All our direct knowledge can be reduced to that which we receive through our senses; from which it follows that we owe all our ideas to our sensations. This principle of the early philosophers was long regarded as axiomatic by the scholastic philosophers. They paid it this respect merely because it was ancient, and they would have defended with equal fervour the notions of substantial forms and occult qualities. Consequently this truth was treated during the renaissance of philosophy in the same way as the absurd opinions from which it should have been distinguished; it was proscribed along with these opinions, for nothing is more dangerous to truth, and nothing exposes it more to misunderstanding than its alliance with or proximity to error. The theory of innate ideas, attractive in several respects, and perhaps the more striking because it was less familiar, took the place of the axiom of the scholastics; it has reigned for a long time and still retains some partisans; such is the difficulty truth has in retaking its proper place when once prejudice or sophistry has expelled it from it. In recent times, however, there has been almost general agreement that the ancients were right; and this is not the only question on which we are beginning to draw near to them again.

Nothing is more certain than the existence of our sensations. Consequently, to prove that they are the origins of all our knowledge, it is sufficient to show that they can be; for, in good philosophy, every inference based on facts or recognized truths is preferable to those grounded only on hypotheses, however ingenious. Why posit that we have purely intellectual notions from the beginning if all we need to do, in order to form them, is to reflect on our sensations? The following details will go to show that these notions have in fact no other origin.

The first thing that our experience teaches us and that indeed cannot be distinguished from them is our existence; from which it follows that our first reflective ideas must be concerned with ourselves, that is to say with that thinking principle which constitutes our nature, and which is in no way different from ourselves. The second thing our sensations teach is the existence of external objects, amongst which our own bodies must be included, since they are external to us, so to speak, even before we have sorted out the nature of the thinking principle within us. These innumerable objects make so forceful and continuous an effect on us, an effect which so binds us to them, that, after a first instance when our reflective ideas make us look into ourselves, we are forced to turn outside by the sensations that assail us from all sides, and that tear us from the solitude in which we would remain without them. The multiplicity of these sensations, the agreement we notice in their evidence, the nuances we observe in them, the involuntary responses they induce in us, compared with the voluntary determination which dictates our reflective ideas and operates only on our sensations themselves; all of these things produce in us an irresistible leaning towards affirming the existence of the objects to which we relate these sensations and which seem to us to be the cause of them. Many philosophers have seen this leaning as the work of a superior being and as the most convincing argument for the existence of these objects. Indeed, as there is no relation between each sensation and the object which occasions it or at least to which we relate it, there does not appear to be any possible passage from one to the other discoverable by reasoning. Only a kind of instinct, surer than reason itself, can force us to clear so great a gap. This instinct is so active in us, that, supposing for a moment that it subsided whilst the external objects were destroyed, the sudden re-creation of these same objects could not intensify its strength. Let us then accept, without hesitation, that our sensations have in fact the cause outside ourselves that we suppose them to have, since the effect which can result from the real existence of that cause could not differ in any way from that which we actually experience; and let us not copy those philosophers of whom Montaigne speaks, who, when asked about the principle of human actions, still question whether men exist. Far from wishing to obscure truths recognized even by the sceptics in their less quarrelsome moments, let us leave to the enlightened metaphysicians the task of developing its principle. It is for them to determine, if this is possible, what gradation our mind observes in that first glance outside itself, pushed, so to speak, and at the same time held back by a host of perceptions that draw it towards external objects on the one hand, and on the other, since these perceptions belong to the mind itself properly speaking, seem to limit it within narrow boundaries from which they do not allow it to emerge.

Of all the objects that affect us by their presence, our own body is that whose existence strikes us most, since it relates to us most closely. But scarcely do we feel the existence of our body than we perceive the demand it makes of us to avoid the dangers that surround it. Subject to a thousand needs and highly sensitive to the action of external objects, it would soon be destroyed if we were not occupied with the task of conserving it. Not that all external bodies create disagreeable sensations in us; some seem to compensate us by the pleasure their action brings to us. But such is the misfortune of the human condition that pain is our most lively sentiment; pleasure moves us less than pain and is almost never sufficient to console us for it. In vain have some philosophers, restraining their cries amidst sufferings, maintained that pain is not an evil: in vain have others placed the supreme happiness in sensual pleasure, from which they nevertheless refrained for fear of the consequences. All would have understood our nature better if they had been content to limit the sovereign good of this life to the exemption from pain, and to agree that we cannot attain this sovereign good but only to approach it nearer or farther in proportion to our vigilance and the care we take. Such natural reflections will inevitably strike every man who is left to himself and is free of the prejudices of both education and study. They follow on the first impression he receives from external objects and can be placed amongst the first movements of the mind, precious to the truly wise and worthy of being observed by them, but neglected or rejected by ordinary philosophy, whose basic principles they almost always contradict.

The necessity of protecting our own bodies from pain and destruction makes us pick out from amongst external objects those which can be useful or harmful to us, in order to pursue the former and avoid the latter. But scarcely have we begun to examine these objects than we discover amongst them a large number of beings who seem to us completely the same as ourselves, that is to say whose form is entirely like ours and who, so far as we can judge at first sight, seem to have the same perceptions as we do. All this leads us to believe that they have also the same needs as we feel and consequently the same interest in satisfying them. From which it follows that we must find it very advantageous to unite with them to find out what is beneficial and what harmful to us in nature.

From Condillac's *Extrait raisonné du traité des sensations*

Locke distinguishes two sources of our ideas, the senses and reflections. It would be more exact to recognize only one, either because reflection is in its origin only sensation itself, or because it is less the source of ideas than the channel through which they flow from the senses.

This mistake, slight though it appears, throws much of his system into obscurity, for it makes him powerless to develop its principles. Also this philosopher is content to accept that the mind perceives, thinks, questions, believes, reasons, knows, wills, reflects, that we are convinced of the existence of these processes since we find them in ourselves, and that they contribute to the growth of our knowledge; but he has not felt the need to discover their origin and generation, he has not suspected that they can be nothing other than acquired habits; he seems to have regarded them as something innate and says only that they perfect themselves by use.

13 La Mettrie and Materialism

Julien Offray de La Mettrie (1709–51) was born at St Malo of wealthy parents. Like so many of the philosophes, he was intended originally for the Church but was attracted to medicine. On his account, he was led to the materialist view that thought is a function of man's physical constitution by recording his own progress through a fever. He put these materialist ideas forward in his L'histoire naturelle de l'âme *(1745) and* L'homme machine *(1748). After the publication of the second, he fled to the court of Frederick the Great to escape arrest.*

From *Histoire naturelle de l'âme*

Neither Aristotle nor Plato nor Descartes nor Malebranche can teach you what your soul is. In vain do you fret about knowing its nature: despite your vanity and indocility, you must resign yourself to ignorance and faith. The essence of the soul of man and animals is and always will be as unknown as the essence of matter and of bodies. I would say more: the soul detached from the body by abstraction is like matter thought of without any form; it is inconceivable. The soul and the body have been made together at the same time, as if by a single stroke of the brush. They have been cast in the same mould, said a great theologian (Tertullian) who did not fear thought. Thus, those who wish to know the properties of the soul must first inquire into those that reveal themselves clearly in bodies, of which the soul is the active principle.

This reflection leads naturally to the thought that there is no more sure guide than the senses. Here are my philosophers. Whatever ill can be said of them, they alone can enlighten the mind in the search for truth; it is to them alone that it is always necessary to return if we wish seriously to know the truth.

Let us then see with as much good faith as impartiality what our senses can discern in matter, in the substance of bodies, and especially organic bodies; but let us see only what is there and imagine nothing. Of itself, matter is a passive principle, it has only a force of inertia; that is why, every time it is seen to move, it can be concluded that its movement comes from another principle, which an honest mind will never confuse with that which contains it, I mean with matter or the substance of bodies, since the idea of the one and the idea of the other form two concepts as different as active and passive. If then there is in bodies a moving principle and if it is proved that the same principle which makes the heart beat also makes the nerves feel and the brain think, does it not clearly follow that it is to this principle we give the name *soul*?

14 D'Holbach and Hedonism

Baron Paul Henri Thiry d'Holbach (1723–89) was born in the Palatinate but settled in Paris in 1749. He inherited his title and considerable wealth from his uncle. Through his friendship with Diderot, he supported and contributed to the Encyclopédie; *initially he wrote scientific articles, but increasingly he was drawn to religious, ethical and social topics. This interest bore fruit in his* Système de la nature *of 1770 in which he laid down the anti-religious and materialist themes he was to develop in his subsequent writings.*

From *The System of Nature*

But what is the end or aim of man in the sphere that he occupies? It is to conserve himself and to render his existence happy. It is then of the utmost importance that he should be acquainted with the true means which his reason and his prudence teaches him to make use of, that he may surely and constantly arrive at the end which he proposes to himself. These means are his natural faculties, his mind—his talents—his industry—his actions determined by the passions of which his Nature renders him susceptible, and which give more or less activity to his will. Experience and reason again show him, that the men with whom he is associated are necessary to him—are capable of contributing to his happiness—to his pleasures—are capable of assisting him by the faculties which are peculiar to them; experience teaches him in what manner he can be able to make them concur in his designs—determine them to will and act in his favour—he sees the actions which they approve, and those which displease them—the conduct which attracts them, and that which repels them—the judgment by which they are swayed—the advantageous or prejudicial effects that result from their different modes of being and of acting. All this experience gives him the idea of virtue and of vice—of justice and of injustice—of goodness and of wicked-ness—of decency and of indecency—of probity and of knavery, etc. etc., in a word, he learns to form a judgment of men and of their actions—to distinguish the necessary sentiments which are excited in them, according to the diversity of the effects that they make them experience.

It is upon the necessary diversity of these effects that is founded the distinction of good and of evil—of vice and of virtue; distinctions which are not, as some thinkers have believed, founded upon the conventions between men, and again much less upon the chimerical will of a super-natural being; but upon the eternal and invariable relations that subsist between the beings of the human species living in society, and which will subsist as long as man and society shall continue to exist. Thus VIRTUE is everything that is truly and constantly useful to the beings of the human species living in society; VICE is everything that is prejudi-cial and injurious to them. The greatest virtues are those which procure them the most durable—the most solid, and the greatest advantages; the greatest vices are those which most disturb their tendency to happ-iness, and the necessary order of society. The VIRTUOUS MAN is him whose actions tend constantly to the well-being and happiness of his fellow creatures; the VICIOUS MAN is him whose conduct tends to the misery and unhappiness of those with whom he lives, from whence his own peculiar misery must most commonly result. Everything that procures us for ourselves a true and permanent happiness is reasonable; everything that disturbs our own peculiar felicity, or that of the beings who are necessary to our happiness, is foolish or unreasonable. A man who injures others is wicked; the man who injures himself is an imprudent being, who neither has a knowledge of reason—nor of his peculiar interests—nor of truth.

Our DUTIES are the means of which experience and reason point out to us the necessity that we may arrive at the end which we propose to ourselves: these duties are a necessary consequence of the relations subsisting between men, who equally desire the happiness and the conservation of their being. When they say that these duties COMPEL US, that only signifies, that without taking these means, we could not be able to arrive at the end which our nature proposes to itself. Thus MORAL OBLIGATION is the necessity of employing the natural means to render the beings with whom we live happy, to the end that we may determine them to contribute to our own happiness; our obligations towards ourselves are the necessity of taking those means, without which we should not be able to conserve ourselves, nor render our existence solidly and permanently happy. Morals, like the universe, is founded upon necessity, or upon the eternal relation of things.

V

Religion

For many thinkers writing in reaction to the French Revolution, the Enlightenment and its brutish revolutionary child were new satanic revolts against God, products of an overweening pride incapable of suffering any authority even that of the Divine Author of the universe. Maistre, who made this accusation most forthrightly (see p. 81), saw the *philosophes*, the tribe of intellectuals, as a conspiracy intent on subverting Christianity; their social and political aims were incidental to this dark purpose, by-products of the fact that European societies and governments rested on Christian foundations. There is at least as good a case for seeing the reverse as true, for arguing that the attack on orthodox religion arose from dislike of the social and political uses to which the power of organized religion was put. Certainly, whilst the *philosophes* were strung along a broad spectrum of religious (and non-religious) beliefs, there was fairly general agreement on the need for toleration. Locke's plea for tolerance by civil powers of a variety of religious opinions was a classic statement of this concern, which was (like much of what Locke wrote) both typical and influential.

Although Locke did not disavow Christian faith, the defence of toleration and the critique of organized Christianity were nurtured in the same soil. Scepticism and the new scientific attitude mingled to create an atmosphere that, at least in France, made the conflict between creeds and sects seem at best irrelevant and at worst, when it was the occasion for cruelty and persecution, immoral. The sceptical tradition, running through writers such as Bayle, Fontenelle and Voltaire, turned the techniques learnt in secular history on to sacred writings, sought to show that moral behaviour did not depend on, did not even result from Christian belief, and, overtly attacking superstition, used arguments which covertly undermined faith. Newtonian physics seemed, at least to Newton himself, to offer a new demonstration of an old argument for the existence of God, the argument from design (see pp. 42–43). This argument became the focal point of deistic thought. Men need only look around them and see the order of the natural world to recognize that there exists an ordering intelligence, a first cause or prime mover that has set the machine in motion. Equally, men need only consult their own hearts or reason to discover the rules of right and wrong; they need no explicit revelation, no clerical intermediary, to guide them. In England, such rationalist and deistic ideas could be at least partly absorbed by a latitudinarian Church. In France, faced with a militant and persecuting Church, deism both attracted more intellectual authority and came into conflict with institutional Christianity. In his article 'Religion', Voltaire moves easily along a line of argument that starts from an organizing intelligence, passes through a universal morality and ends in the iniquities of Christian sects (see pp. 43–45). It is this end-point that links Voltaire with the atheists. The materialism of thinkers such as La Mettrie and d'Holbach pushed them much further than Voltaire was willing to go; but, as the extract from *Le bon sens* shows, they too were deeply, perhaps primarily, concerned with the tyranny, cruelty and ignorance which they believed were perpetuated by religious beliefs and authorities (see pp. 45–46). This protest, and this protest alone, united Enlightenment thinkers in their religious attitudes. Helvétius's dialogue between a deist and an atheist reflects an argument that divided them (see pp. 47–49).

15 Locke on Toleration

From *A Letter Concerning Toleration*

The commonwealth seems to me to be a society of men constituted only for the procuring, preserving, and advancing their own civil interests.

Civil interests I call life, liberty, health, and indolency of body; and the possession of outward things, such as money, lands, houses, furniture, and the like.

It is the duty of the civil magistrate, by the impartial execution of equal laws, to secure unto all the people in general, and to every one of his subjects in particular, the just possession of these things belonging to this life. If anyone presume to violate the laws of public justice and equity, established for the preservation of those things, his presumption is to be checked by the fear of punishment consisting of the deprivation or diminution of those civil interests or goods which otherwise he might and ought to enjoy. But seeing no man does willingly suffer himself to be punished by the deprivation of any part of his goods, and much less of his liberty or life, therefore is the magistrate armed with the force and strength of all his subjects, in order to the punishment of those that violate any other man's rights.

Now that the whole jurisdiction of the magistrate reaches only to these civil concernments; and that all civil power, right and dominion is bounded and confined to the only care of promoting these things; and that it neither can nor ought in any manner to be extended to the salvation of souls, these following considerations seem unto me abundantly to demonstrate.

First, because the care of souls is not committed to the civil magistrate any more than to other men. It is not committed unto him, I say, by God; because it appears not that God has ever given any such authority to one man over another, as to compel anyone to his religion. Nor can any such power be vested in the magistrate by the consent of the people, because no man can so far abandon the care of his own salvation as blindly to leave to the choice of any other, whether prince or subject, to prescribe to him what faith or worship he shall embrace. . . .

In the second place, the care of souls cannot belong to the civil magistrate because his power consists only in outward force; but true and saving religion consists in the inward persuasion of the mind, without which nothing can be acceptable to God. And such is the nature of the understanding that it cannot be compelled to the belief of anything by outward force. Confiscation of estate, imprisonment, torments, nothing of that nature can have any such efficacy as to make men change the inward judgment that they have framed of things.

It may indeed be alleged that the magistrate may make use of arguments, and thereby draw the heterodox into the way of truth and procure their salvation. I grant it; but this is common to him with other men. . . .

In the third place, the care of the salvation of men's souls cannot belong to the magistrate; because, though the rigor of laws and the force of penalties were capable to convince and change men's minds, yet would not that help at all to the salvation of their souls. For there being but one truth, one way to heaven, what hope is there that more men would be led into it if they had no rule but the religion of the court, and were put under the necessity to quit the light of their own reason, and oppose the dictates of their own consciences, and blindly to resign themselves up to the will of their governors and to the religion which either ignorance, ambition, or superstition had chanced to establish in the countries where they were born? In the variety and contradiction of opinions in religion, wherein the princes of the world are as much divided as in their secular interests, the narrow way would be much straitened; one country alone would be in the right, and all the rest of the world put under an obligation of following their princes in the ways that lead to destruction; and that which heightens the absurdity, and very ill suits the notion of a Deity, men would owe their eternal happiness or misery to the places of their nativity.

These considerations, to omit many others that might have been urged to the same purpose, seem unto me sufficient to conclude that all the power of civil government relates only to men's civil interests, is confined to the care of the things of this world, and hath nothing to do with the world to come.

16 Newton and the Argument from Design

From *Optics*

The main business of natural philosophy is to argue from phenomena without feigning hypotheses and to deduce causes from effects, till we come to the very first cause, which certainly is not mechanical; and not only to unfold the mechanism of the world, but chiefly to resolve these and suchlike questions. What is there in places almost empty of matter, and whence is it that the sun and planets gravitate toward one another, without dense matter between them? Whence is it that nature does nothing in vain, and whence arises all that order and beauty which we see in the world? To what end are comets, and whence is it that planets move all one and the same way in orbs concentric while comets move all manner of ways in orbs very eccentric, and what hinders the fixed stars from falling upon one another? How came the bodies of animals to be contrived with so much art, and for what ends were their several parts? Was the eye contrived without skill in optics and the ear without knowledge of sounds? How do the motions of the body follow from the will, and whence is the instinct in animals? Is not the sensory of animals that place to which the sensitive substance is present and into which the sensible species of things are carried through the nerves and brain, that there they may be perceived by their immediate presence to that substance? And these things being rightly dispatched, does it not appear from phenomena that there is a Being, incorporeal, living, intelligent, omnipresent, who in infinite space, as it were in his sensory, sees the things themselves intimately and thoroughly perceives them, and comprehends them wholly by their immediate presence to himself, of which things the images only carried through the organs of sense into our little sensoriums are there seen and beheld by that which in us perceives and thinks? And though every true step made in this philosophy brings us not immediately to the knowledge of the first cause, yet it brings us nearer to it, and on that account is to be highly valued.

17 Voltaire's Deism

From the article 'Religion' in *Questions sur l'encyclopédie*

I have been meditating this night; I have been sunk in the contemplation of nature; I have been admiring the immensity, the movement, the interrelations of those endless globes that the masses do not know how to admire.

I have been admiring still more the intelligence that watches over this immense complex. I said to myself: 'One would have to be blind not to be dazzled by this sight; one would have to be stupid not to recognize its author; one would have to be mad not to worship him. What tribute of adoration ought I to offer to him? Ought not this tribute to be the same throughout the whole extent of space, since the same supreme sovereign reigns in the same way throughout this space? Does not a thinking being inhabiting a star in the Milky Way owe the same homage to Him as a thinking being on this small globe of ours? The light is no different on Sirius than on earth; morality ought to be the same. If a feeling and thinking animal on Sirius is born of a tender father and mother who have been concerned with his welfare, he owes as much love and solicitude to them as we owe here to our parents. If someone in the Milky Way sees a maimed beggar, if he can succour him and fails to do so, he is guilty on every star. The heart has everywhere the same duties, on the steps of God's throne, if He has a throne, and at the bottom of the abyss, if there is an abyss.'

I was plunged in these thoughts when one of those spirits who fill the empty spaces of the universe came down to me. I recognized this same aerial creature as the one who had appeared to me in the past to teach me how the judgments of God differ from ours and how a good action is preferable to a bad one.

He carried me to a desert completely covered in piled-up bones; and between these heaps of skeletons there were avenues of trees always in leaf. . . .

'Alas, archangel,' I said to him, 'where have you led me?'

'To desolation,' he replied. . . .

He started with the first heap.

'These are the twenty-three thousand Jews who danced before a calf, together with twenty-four thousand who were killed over the Medean women. The number of those massacred for such offences or mistakes add up to close on three hundred thousand. By the next avenues are the charnel-houses of Christians who have butchered each other for metaphysical disputes. They are divided into different piles each of four centuries. A single pile would have reached to heaven, and it has been necessary to divide them.'

'What!' I cried. 'Brothers have treated their brothers thus, and I have the misfortune to be one of the brotherhood!'

'Here,' said the spirit, 'are the twelve million American Indians killed in their native land because they had not been baptised.'

'My God! Why do you not leave these hideous remains to waste away in the hemisphere in which their bodies were born and where they were subject to so many different deaths? Why bring together all these abominable memorials to barbarism and fanaticism?'

'To instruct you.'

'Since you wish to instruct me,' I said to the spirit, 'tell me if there have been peoples other than Christians and Jews in whom zeal and religion, unfortunately transformed into fanaticism, have inspired so much horrible cruelty.'

'Yes,' he said to me, 'the Mohammedans have tainted themselves with the same inhumanities, but only rarely; and, when tribute has been offered to them, they have granted pardon. As for other nations, there has not been one since the beginning of the world which has ever waged a purely religious war. Now follow me.'

I followed him.

44

A little beyond these piles of the dead, we found other piles: they were of bags of gold and silver, and each had its own label—'Wealth of heretics massacred in the eighteenth century, in the seventeenth century, in the sixteenth century', and further on thus, 'Gold and silver of slaughtered Americans, etc., etc.' And all these piles were topped by crosses, mitres, bishop's crooks, tiaras enriched with precious stones.

'Why, was it then to gain these riches that these corpses have been amassed?'

'Yes, my son.'

18 D'Holbach's Atheism

From *Le bon sens*

When men's opinions are looked at calmly, it is very surprising to find that, even in those which they regard as most essential, nothing is rarer than to see them make use of good sense, that is to say that part of judgment sufficient to appreciate the simplest truths, to reject the most obvious absurdities, to be offended by palpable contradictions. We have an example of this in Theology, a science revered at all times, in all countries and by the majority of men, a subject they regard as the most important, the most useful, the most indispensable to the welfare of societies. In fact, if one takes the trouble to probe the principles on which this so-called science rests, one is forced to recognize that these principles, regarded as incontestable, are only rash assumptions, dreamed up by ignorance, propagated by enthusiasm on bad faith, adopted by timid credulity, preserved by unreasoning habit and revered only because it is not understood. . . .

In a word, whoever deigns to consult good sense about religious beliefs and brings to this scrutiny the attention ordinarily given to subjects accepted as important will easily perceive that these beliefs have no solid foundations, that every religion is a castle in the air, that Theology is nothing but ignorance of natural causes reduced to a system, that it is only a long tissue of fancies and contradictions, that, in every country and to the different peoples of the world, it offers nothing but improbable romances, whose hero himself is made up of an impossible combination of qualities; his name, capable of exciting respect and fear in every heart, will be found to be only a vague word that men have continually on their lips without being able to attach to it any ideas or qualities that are not belied by the facts or are not obviously self-contradictory.

The notion of this incomprehensible Being, or rather the word by which it is designated, would be of little importance if it did not give rise to countless ravages on the earth. Seized by the idea that this phantom is a reality of concern to all men, rather than concluding wisely that it is incomprehensible and that they can legitimately dismiss it, they conclude on the contrary that they cannot occupy themselves sufficiently with it, that they must meditate on it without pause, argue about it without end and never lose it from sight. Their invincible ignorance in this respect, far from discouraging them, serves only to excite their curiosity: rather than putting them on guard against their imagination, this ignorance makes them peremptory, dogmatic, domineering, and leads them to get angry with all those who oppose some doubts to the dreams spawned by their minds.

What perplexity, when it is a question of resolving an insoluble problem! Uneasy meditations on a subject which is impossible to grasp and yet which he supposes concerns him deeply can only disturb man's temper and produce dangerous passions in his head. If self-interest, vanity and ambition come to join this troubled frame of mind, society must be shaken. This is why so many nations have often become stages for the follies of a few mad dreamers, who, extolling or claiming their futile speculations as eternal truths, have inflamed the fanaticism of princes and peoples and armed them for opinions which they represent to them as essential to the glory of the Divinity and the happiness of empires. A thousand times, on every part of one globe, there have been fanatics drunk with the desire to slit each other's throats, to light the stakes, to commit the greatest crimes without scruple and for duty's sake, to make human blood flow. Why? To maintain or propagate the impertinent conjectures of a few fanatics, or to accredit the deceits of a few imposters about a Being which exists only in their imagination and which makes itself known only by the ravages, disputes and follies that it has brought about on the earth.

19 Helvétius's Conversation between a Deist and an Atheist

Claude Adrien Helvétius (1715–71) had the good fortune to be appointed a tax farmer at the age of twenty-three and was thus able to retire rich eleven years later in order to devote himself to writing. His De l'esprit, *a statement of materialist and utilitarian doctrine, was denounced by the Sorbonne, condemned by the Paris* Parlement *to be publicly burned and was consequently very widely read. He was forced to retract but his views were repeated in* De l'homme *published in 1772 after his death.*

From *Les progrès de la raison dans la recherche du vrai*

THE ATHEIST

The dispute between us can be reduced to whether eternal nature acts with wisdom and design or whether it takes all sorts of forms through blind necessity. Let us not confuse ourselves with vulgar prejudices. A philosopher should believe only when he is forced to it by overwhelming proof. I reason only on the basis of what I see, and, in the whole of nature, I see nothing but immeasurable matter and a boundless force. This active matter is eternal. Now, in an infinite space of time, an omnipotent force must necessarily give every kind of form to immeasurable matter. It has had other forms than those we see today; it will take yet others in the future. All has changed, all is changing, all will change. This is the eternal circle in which atoms revolve.

THE DEIST

This is a sophism and not a proof. You say that you see, in the whole of nature, nothing but boundless force and immeasurable matter. I agree; but does it follow that the boundless force is a property of matter? Matter is eternal, you add; this may be so, because the boundless force, continually active, has been able to produce it at all times: but do you conclude from this that it is the sole existing substance? I would agree further that the omnipotent force can give, in an infinite time, every kind of form to immeasurable matter; but is this proof that this force acts through blind necessity and without design? While I would admit your principles, yet I would deny the consequences you draw from them, for they appear to me absolutely false. And here is the reason:

The idea we have of light does not include that of force. It must be matter when it is in a state of perfect rest; it cannot yield movement when it has lost it. From this, I conclude that it is not active of itself, and consequently that boundless force is not one of its properties.

Moreover, I perceive in myself, and in a number of beings which surround me, a comparative principle that feels, reasons and judges. Now it is absurd to imagine that matter without thought and feeling can feel and become intelligent by changing its location or its shape; there is no connection between these ideas. It is true that the intensity of our feelings often depends on the movement of our humours; this proves that the mind and the body can be united, but by no means that they are one. From this I conclude that there is in nature a substance other than matter, and consequently that there must be a sovereign intelligence far superior to my mind, to your mind, to all men's minds.

To know if there is such an intelligence, I pass my eye over all the marvels of the universe. I observe the constancy and regularity of its laws, the fecundity and variety of its products, the harmony and conformity of its parts, the constitution of animals, the structure of plants, the order of the elements, the movement of stars: then I can no longer doubt that everything is the effect of a purpose, an art and a supreme wisdom. From this I conclude that the boundless force that you recognize in nature is a sovereign and omnipotent intelligence.

A superficial glance at these wonders might leave the mind in uncertainty; but when one enters into the sanctuary of nature, when one studies its secrets in depth, hesitation is no longer possible. I do not see how the atheist can resist the force of these arguments.

Now that I have given you the reasons which lead me to believe, I pray you tell me more that can make you doubt.

THE ATHEIST

An infinitely wise and powerful Being should embody every kind of perfection; his goodness and justice ought to equal his wisdom and power; yet the world is full of defects and vices. Everywhere I see unhappy and wicked beings. Now I cannot conceive how sufferings and crimes can start or continue under the rule of a supremely good, wise and powerful Being. The idea of an infinitely perfect cause seems to me incompatible with beings so contrary to his beneficent nature. This is the reason for my doubts.

THE DEIST

What! Do you deny what you see clearly because you can see no further? The smallest light carries us to belief; but the deepest obscurity is no reason for denying. In this twilight of human life, the lights of the mind are too weak to reveal to us the primary truths in perfect clearness. They may only be glimpsed from afar by a stray beam which is sufficient to guide us; but this does not give sufficient light to dissipate all shadows. Would you reject the most convincing proof of a sovereign Intelligence because you do not see the hidden reasons for his conduct? You deny the eternal Wisdom because you do not understand how evil can exist under his empire. Is this rational? A thing does not exist because you do not see it: this is what all your objections boil down to.

The desire to penetrate and understand all things, to adjust everything to our imperfect ideas, is the most dangerous malady of the human mind. The most exalted effort of our reason is to keep silent before the sovereign reason. Let us leave to the supreme Intelligence the task of justifying one day the inscrutable ways of Providence. Our pride and our impatience make us unwilling to await this outcome; we wish to outstrip the light, and we lose it from sight.

Without the idea of an omnipotent Intelligence, real happiness is a contradiction. Far from being able to find his happiness by himself, man alone cannot but be miserable, imperfect, weak and limited; stirred by a thousand desires far beyond his power, how could he delude himself that he is happy without the aid of a Being completely wise to enlighten our minds, all-powerful to alleviate our weakness, and infinitely perfect to make good our imperfections? If such a Being did not exist, man would be the most unhappy of all the creatures existing on the earth: for he carries within himself all the causes of his misery, which is not the case with other animals.

VI

Optimism and the Problem of Evil

Do earthly evils exist through God's wishes? Then God is malevolent. Does evil exist despite God's wishes? Then God is not omnipotent. The realization of this dilemma was not of course novel to the Enlightenment. But 'Epicurus's old questions', in Hume's phrase, presented themselves anew to the age of reason with a special poignancy and urgency. To rational and freshly scientific men, the Christian explanations—original sin, the fall, the devil, rewards and punishments in another world—were losing their conviction. How then to explain the undeniable facts? One answer very commonly accepted in the early eighteenth century was the theory of optimism, derived largely from Leibniz. The name is somewhat misleading, for optimism did not deny the reality of evil nor did it promise any amelioration in the human condition. When it was attacked, as it was by Voltaire, the targets were precisely its lack of protest or hope, its intolerable acceptance of the intolerable, its bland justification of the burdens pressing on humanity. What the theory did offer was an explanation of evil not a programme for its elimination. Its claim that this is the best of all possible worlds, so ruthlessly parodied by Voltaire in *Candide*, did not imply that all evil was, properly viewed, good, but that evil was a necessary part of any metaphysically conceivable world. No possible universe could be without evil, but, of all possible universes, this is the one with the most favourable balance of good and evil. Amongst the most popular and influential expressions of this theory was Pope's *Essay on Man*. It has been argued that there are important differences between Pope's optimism and that of Leibniz (see p. 159); but the final message of the *Essay* is also a quietist call to acceptance. 'To reason right is to submit.'

Although the materialists denied the meaningfulness of the problem of evil, their argument paralleled that of the optimists. The universe, a mechanism subject to inevitable natural laws, could not be judged in moral terms. This was not the best of all possible worlds, for there was only one possible world; but all in it was necessary. The end of this argument, as with optimism, was a justification of what is.

Voltaire opened fire on both these positions in his poem on the Lisbon earthquake of 1755, a traumatic experience which raised in their acutest forms all the questions of the problem of evil. His target was not only the axiom, *tout est bien*, but also *ces immuables lois de la nécessité*. However, his vigorous critique is not supported by any strong alternative solution. He held out no explanation, only the hope, *un jour tout sera bien*. To this belief men must hold to save themselves from a world without God or a world under a cruel God.

Un jour tout sera bien; but, in Voltaire's poem, this is a cry of faith not a call to action. There is no reason given why this hope should be fulfilled, no programme pointed out by which its realization could be ensured. Other writers proferred an explanation if not of physical ills then of moral ills, of man's inhumanity to man. It was, claimed Diderot and Rousseau, society itself that had corrupted man. Men were not originally sinful, they were not moral centaurs, corrupt and divided by nature. The gap between their intentions and their actions, their nature and their performance, between what they feel they can be and what they know they are, had been created by a division between the moral feelings engraven on their hearts and the behaviour and attitudes forced on them by society. This still left the question of how this fateful degeneration had come about. D'Holbach gave a clear, perhaps crude but pregnant answer—it had happened because kings and priests had distorted laws and obscured men's minds to further their own interests. The theory of conspiracy entered as a solution of the paradox of moral man in immoral society.

The problem of evil was a subject that fascinated and frightened the eighteenth-century mind. The sombre tone of this concern reverberates too often to justify the common picture of the period as one of thoughtless and naïve buoyancy. Yet the reduction of the problem (or at least part of it) to social and political terms transformed it. What had previously been a matter of explanation and understanding now became a subject of planning and action.

20 Hume and the Problem of Evil

From *Dialogues Concerning Natural Religion*

... The miseries of life, the unhappiness of man, the general corruptions of our nature, the unsatisfactory enjoyment of pleasures, riches, honours; these phrases have become almost proverbial in all languages. And who can doubt of what all men declare from their own immediate feeling and experience?

In this point, said PHILO, the learned are perfectly agreed with the vulgar; and in all letters, *sacred* and *profane*, the topic of human misery has been insisted on with the most pathetic eloquence that sorrow and melancholy could inspire. The poets, who speak from sentiment, without a system, and whose testimony has therefore the more authority, abound in images of this nature. From HOMER down to DR YOUNG, the whole inspired tribe have ever been sensible, that no other representation of things would suit the feeling and observation of each individual.

As to authorities, replied DEMEA, you need not seek them. Look round this library of CLEANTHES. I shall venture to affirm, that, except authors of particular sciences, such as chemistry or botany, who have no occasion to treat of human life, there scarce is one of those innumerable writers, from whom the sense of human misery has not, in some passage or other, extorted a complaint and confession of it. At least, the chance is entirely on that side; and no one author has ever, so far as I can recollect, been so extravagant as to deny it.

There you must excuse me, said PHILO: LEIBNITZ has denied it; and is perhaps the first, who ventured upon so bold and paradoxical an opinion; at least, the first, who made it essential to his philosophical system.

And by being the first, replied DEMEA, might he not have been sensible of his error? For is this a subject in which philosophers can propose to make discoveries, especially in so late an age? And can any man hope by a simple denial (for the subject scarcely admits of reasoning) to bear down the united testimony of mankind, founded on sense and consciousness?

And why should man, added he, pretend to an exemption from the lot of all other animals? The whole earth, believe me, PHILO, is cursed and polluted. A perpetual war is kindled amongst all living creatures. Necessity, hunger, want, stimulate the strong and courageous: Fear, anxiety, terror, agitate the weak and infirm. The first entrance into life gives anguish to the new-born infant and to its wretched parent: Weakness, impotence, distress, attend each stage of that life: And it is at last finished in agony and horror. . . .

And it is possible, CLEANTHES, said PHILO, that after all these reflections, and infinitely more, which might be suggested, you can still persevere in your anthropomorphism, and assert the moral attributes of the Deity, his justice, benevolence, mercy, and rectitude, to be of the same nature with these virtues in human creatures? His power we allow infinite: Whatever he wills is executed: But neither man nor any other animal are happy: Therefore he does not will their happiness. His wisdom is infinite: He is never mistaken in choosing the means to any end: But the course of nature tends not to human or animal felicity: Therefore it is not established for that purpose. Through the whole compass of human knowledge, there are no inferences more certain and infallible than these. In what respect, then, do his benevolence and mercy resemble the benevolence and mercy of men?

EPICURUS's old questions are yet unanswered. Is he willing to prevent evil, but not able? then is he impotent. Is he able, but not willing? then is he malevolent. Is he both able and willing? whence then is evil?

21 Whatever is, is Right: Pope

Alexander Pope (1688–1744) published his Essay on Man *in 1733. The philosophy expressed in it was influenced as much by Shaftesbury and Bolingbroke as by Leibniz.*

From *An Essay on Man*

> Ask for what end the heavenly bodies shine,
> Earth for whose use? Pride answers, ' 'Tis for mine:
> For me kind nature wakes her genial pow'r,
> Suckles each herb, and spreads out every flow'r:
> Annual for me, the grape, the rose renew
> The juice nectareous, and the balmy dew;
> For me, the mine a thousand treasures brings;
> For me, health gushes from a thousand springs;

Seas roll to waft me, suns to light me rise;
My footstool earth, my canopy the skies.'
    But errs not Nature from this gracious end,
From burning suns when livid deaths descend,
When earthquakes swallow, or when tempests sweep
Towns to one grave, whole nations to the deep?
'No ('tis replied), the first Almighty Cause
Acts not by partial, but by gen'ral laws;
The exceptions few; some change since all began:
And what created perfect?'—Why then Man?
If the great end be human happiness,
Then nature deviates; and can man do less?
As much that end a constant course requires
Of show'rs and sunshine, as of man's desires;
As much eternal springs and cloudless skies,
As men for ever temperate, calm, and wise.
If plagues or earthquakes break not Heaven's design,
Why then a Borgia, or a Catiline?
Who know but He, whose hand the lightning forms,
Who heaves old ocean, and who wings the storms;
Pours fierce ambition in a Caesar's mind
Or turns young Ammon loose to scourge mankind?
From pride, from pride, our very reas'ning springs;
Account for moral, as for natural things:
Why charge we Heav'n in those, in these acquit?
In both to reason right is to submit.
    Better for us, perhaps, it might appear,
Were there all harmony, all virtue here;
That never air or ocean felt the wind;
That never passion discomposed the mind.
But all subsists by elemental strife;
And passions are the elements of life.
The gen'ral order, since the whole began,
Is kept in nature, and is kept in man. . . .
    See, through this air, this ocean, and this earth,
All matter quick, and bursting into birth.
Above, how high, progressive life may go!
Around, how wide! how deep extend below!
Vast chain of being! which from God began,
Natures ethereal, human, angel, man,

Beast, bird, fish, insect, what no eye can see,
No glass can reach; from infinite to thee,
From thee to nothing.—On superior pow'rs
Were we to press, inferior might on ours:
Or in the full creation leave a void,
Where, one step broken, the great scale's destroyed:
From Nature's chain whatever link you strike,
Tenth, or ten thousandth, breaks the chain alike.

And, if each system in gradation roll
Alike essential to the amazing whole,
The least confusion but in one, not all
That system only, but the whole must fall.
Let earth unbalanced from her orbit fly,
Planets and suns run lawless through the sky;
Let ruling angels from their spheres be hurled,
Being on being wrecked, and world on world;
Heav'n's whole foundations to their centre nod,
And nature trembles to the throne of God.
All this dread order break—for whom? for thee?
Vile worm!—Oh, madness! pride! impiety!

What if the foot, ordained the dust to tread,
Or hand, to toil, aspired to be the head?
What if the head, the eye, or ear repined
To serve mere engines to the ruling mind?
Just as absurd for any part to claim
To be another, in this general frame
Just as absurd to mourn the tasks or pains,
The great directing mind of all ordains.

All are but parts of one stupendous whole,
Whose body Nature is, and God the soul;
That, changed through all, and yet in all the same;
Great in the earth, as in the ethereal frame;
Warms in the sun, refreshes in the breeze,
Glows in the stars, and blossoms in the trees,
Lives through all life, extends through all extent,
Spreads undivided, operates unspent;
Breathes in our soul, informs our mortal part,
As full, as perfect, in a hair as heart:
As full, as perfect, in vile man that mourns,
As the rapt seraph that adores and burns:

To him no high, no low, no great, no small;
He fills, he bounds, connects, and equals all.
  Cease then, nor order imperfection name:
Our proper bliss depends on what we blame.
Know thy own point: this kind, this due degree
Of blindness, weakness, Heav'n bestows on thee.
Submit.—In this, or any other sphere,
Secure to be as blest as thou canst bear:
Safe in the hand of one disposing power,
Or in the natal, or the mortal hour.
All nature is but art, unknown to thee;
All chance, direction, which thou canst not see;
All discord, harmony not understood;
All partial evil, universal good:
And, spite of pride, in erring reason's spite,
One truth is clear, Whatever is, is right.

22 *Tout est Bien*: Voltaire

From *Poème sur le désastre de Lisbonne*

O malheureux mortels! ô terre déplorable!
O de tous les mortels assemblage effroyable!
D'inutiles douleurs éternel entretien!
Philosophes trompés qui criez: 'Tout est bien';
Accourez, contemplez ces ruines affreuses,
Ces débris, ces lambeaux, ces cendres malheureuses,
Ces femmes, ces enfants l'un sur l'autre entassés,
Sous ces marbres rompus ces membres dispersés;
Cent mille infortunés que la terre dévore,
Qui, sanglants, déchirés, et palpitants encore,
Enterrés sous leurs toits, terminent sans secours
Dans l'horreur des tourments leurs lamentables jours!
Aux cris demi-formés de leurs voix expirantes,
Au spectacle effrayant de leurs cendres fumantes,
Direz-vous: 'C'est l'effet des éternelles lois
Qui d'un Dieu libre et bon nécessitent le choix'?

Direz-vous, en voyant cet amas de victimes:
'Dieu s'est vengé, leur mort est le prix de leurs crimes'?
Quel crime, quelle faute ont commis ces enfants
Sur le sein maternel écrasés et sanglants?
Lisbonne, qui n'est plus, eut-elle plus de vices
Que Londres, que Paris, plongés dans les délices?
Lisbonne est abîmée, et l'on danse à Paris.
Tranquilles spectateurs, intrépides esprits,
De vos frères mourants contemplant les naufrages,
Vous recherchez en paix les causes des orages:
Mais du sort ennemi quand vous sentez les coups,
Devenus plus humains, vous pleurez comme nous.
Croyez-moi, quand la terre entrouvre ses abîmes,
Ma plainte est innocente et mes cris légitimes.
Partout environnés des cruautés du sort,
Des fureurs des méchants, des pièges de la mort,
De tous les éléments éprouvant les atteintes,
Compagnons de nos maux, permettez-nous les plaintes.
C'est l'orgueil, dites-vous, l'orgueil séditieux,
Qui prétend qu'étant mal, nous pouvions être mieux.
Allez interroger les rivages du Tage;
Fouillez dans les débris de ce sanglant ravage;
Demandez aux mourants, dans ce séjour d'effroi,
Si c'est l'orgueil qui crie: 'O ciel, secourez-moi!
O ciel, ayez pitié de l'humaine misère!'
'Tout est bien, dites-vous, et tout est nécessaire.'
Quoi! l'univers entier, sans ce gouffre infernal,
Sans engloutir Lisbonne, eût-il été plus mal?
Êtes-vous assurés que la cause éternelle
Qui fait tout, qui sait tout, qui créa tout pour elle,
Ne pouvait nous jeter dans ces tristes climats
Sans former des volcans allumés sous nos pas?
Borneriez-vous ainsi la suprême puissance?
Lui défendriez-vous d'exercer sa clémence?
L'éternel artisan n'a-t-il pas dans ses mains
Des moyens infinis tout prêts pour ses desseins?
Je désire humblement, sans offenser mon maître,
Que ce gouffre enflammé de soufre et de salpêtre
Eût allumé ses feux dans le fond des déserts.
Je respecte mon Dieu, mais j'aime l'univers.

Quand l'homme ose gémir d'un fléau si terrible,
Il n'est point orgueilleux, hélas! Il est sensible.

. . .

  Non, ne présentez plus à mon cœur agité
Ces immuables lois de la nécessité,
Cette chaîne des corps, des esprits, et des mondes.
O rêves des savants! ô chimères profondes!
Dieu tient en main la chaîne, et n'est point enchaîné;
Par son choix bienfaisant tout est déterminé:
Il est libre, il est juste, il n'est point implacable.
Pourquoi donc souffrons-nous sous un maître équitable?
Voilà le nœud fatal qu'il fallait délier.
Guérirez-vous nos maux en osant les nier?
Tous les peuples, tremblant sous une main divine,
Du mal que vous niez ont cherché l'origine.
Si l'éternelle loi qui meut les éléments
Fait tomber les rochers sous les efforts des vents,
Si les chênes touffus par la foudre s'embrasent,
Ils ne ressentent point des coups qui les écrasent:
Mais je vis, mais je sens, mais mon cœur opprimé
Demande des secours au Dieu qui l'a formé.

. . .

  Que peut donc de l'esprit la plus vaste étendue?
Rien; le livre du sort se ferme à notre vue.
L'homme, étranger à soi, de l'homme est ignoré.
Que suis-je, où suis-je, où vais-je, et d'où suis-je tiré?
Atomes tourmentés sur cet amas de boue,
Que la mort engloutit et dont le sort se joue,
Mais atomes pensants, atomes dont les yeux,
Guidés par la pensée, ont mesuré les cieux;
Au sein de l'infini nous élançons notre être,
Sans pouvoir un moment nous voir et nous connaître.
Ce monde, ce théâtre et d'orgueil et d'erreur,
Est plein d'infortunés qui parlent de bonheur.
Tout se plaint, tout gémit en cherchant le bien-être:
Nul ne voudrait mourir, nul ne voudrait renaître.
Quelquefois, dans nos jours consacrés aux douleurs,
Par la main du plaisir nous essuyons nos pleurs;

Mais le plaisir s'envole, et passe comme une ombre;
Nos chagrins, nos regrets, nos pertes, sont sans nombre.
Le passé n'est pour nous qu'un triste souvenir;
Le présent est affreux, s'il n'est point d'avenir,
Si la nuit du tombeau détruit l'être qui pense.
Un jour tout sera bien, voilà notre espérance;
Tout est bien aujourd'hui, voilà l'illusion.
Les sages me trompaient, et Dieu seul a raison.
Humble dans mes soupirs, soumis dans ma souffrance,
Je ne m'élève point contre la Providence.
Sur un ton moins lugubre on me vit autrefois
Chanter des doux plaisirs les séduisantes lois:
D'autres temps, d'autres mœurs: instruit par la vieillesse,
Des humains égarés partageant la faiblesse,
Dans une épaisse nuit cherchant a m'éclairer,
Je ne sais que souffrir, et non pas murmurer.
  Un calife autrefois, à son heure dernière,
Au Dieu qu'il adorait dit pour toute prière:
'Je t'apporte, ô seul roi, seul être illimité,
Tout ce que tu n'as pas dans ton immensité,
Les défauts, les regrets, les maux et l'ignorance.'
Mais il pouvait encore ajouter *l'espérance*.

23 Corruption by Society

*Denis Diderot (1713–84) was born to middle-class parents in Langres. He
studied in Paris and remained there, for long engaged in literary hack work.
In 1746 he published his* Pensées philosophiques, *which was burned by*
Parlement, *and in 1749 he brought out his* Lettres sur les aveugles, *for
which he was imprisoned. His most important achievement came with the
invitation by the bookseller Le Breton to edit an expanded version of*
Chambers's Cyclopaedia. *Diderot transformed the character of the* Encyclopédie, *enlisting the aid of nearly all the important writers of the time. The
cares of this project, caused as much by his publisher, contributors and friends
as by the authorities, occupied him for nearly two decades. The* Supplément
au voyage de Bougainville *was written in 1772, but appeared in print only
in 1796.*

From Diderot's *Supplément au voyage de Bougainville*

B.   If the laws are good, morals are good; if the laws are bad, morals are bad; if the laws, good or bad, are not observed, the worst condition of a society, there are no morals. Now, how can you hope for laws to be observed when they contradict each other? Run through the history of the ages and of nations both ancient and modern, and you will find men subject to three codes, the code of nature, the civil code and the religious code, and compelled alternately to break these three codes, which have never been in agreement; thus it has come about that there has not been in any country . . . either a man or a citizen or a religious person.

A.   From which no doubt you conclude that, by founding morality on those eternal relations which subsist between men, the law of religion becomes perhaps superfluous; and that the civil law ought not to be anything other than the enunciation of this law of nature.

B.   And this, under the penalty of increasing the wicked rather than making the good.

A.   Or that, if it is thought necessary to preserve all three, the last two must be only exact copies of the first, which we carry engraved at the bottom of our hearts and which will always be the strongest.

B.   This is not quite the case. At birth, we have only a similarity of organization with other beings, the same needs, attraction towards the same pleasures, a common aversion for the same pains: this is what makes man what he is and what should be the basis of the morality which suits him.

A.   That is not easy.

B.   It is so difficult that I readily believe the most uncivilized people on the earth, the Tahitians who hold scrupulously to the law of nature, to be nearer to a good system of laws than any civilized people.

A.   Because it is easier for them to rid themselves of their excessive simplicity than for us to retrace our steps and reform our abuses . . .

B.   Do you want to know the abridged history of all our misery? Here it is. There existed a natural man; within this man, there has been introduced an artificial man; and civil war has been started in men's breasts that lasts the whole of their lives. Sometimes the natural man is the stronger, at other times he is crushed by the moral and artificial man; and, in both cases, the unhappy monster is torn, tortured, tormented, stretched out on the rack; ceaselessly groaning, ceaselessly miserable, either because a false enthusiasm for glory transports and intoxicates him or because a false shame subdues and humbles him.

From D'Holbach's *Le bon sens*

How could the human mind, haunted by frightening phantoms and guided by men interested in perpetuating its ignorance, make any progress? Man has been forced to vegetate in his primitive stupidity; he has been told only about invisible powers on which his fate was supposed to depend. Completely occupied with his fears and his senseless reveries, he has always been at the mercy of his priests who reserve for themselves the right to think for him and to regulate his conduct.

Thus man has been and has always remained an infant without experience, a slave without courage, a fool who has feared to reason and has never extricated himself from the labyrinth in which his ancestors had been lost. He believed himself forced to groan under the yoke of his gods, whom he knew only through the fabulous accounts of their ministers; the latter, having pinioned him with the bonds of opinion, have remained his masters, or rather have loosed him defenceless to the absolute power of tyrants, no less terrible than the gods, whose representatives on earth they were.

Crushed under the double yoke of the spiritual and temporal powers, it has been impossible for peoples to instruct themselves or to work for their happiness. As religion, politics and morals became sanctuaries which the profane were not permitted to enter, men had no other morals than those their rulers and priests caused to come down from the unknown regions of the Empyrean. The human mind, confused by theological opinions, failed to recognize itself, doubted its own powers, mistrusted experience, feared the truth, scorned its reason, and passed it by in order blindly to follow authority. Man was a simple machine in the hands of his tyrants and his priests, who alone had the right to regulate his movements: treated always as a slave, he has had almost at every time and in every place the vices and character of a slave.

These are the real sources of the corruption of customs, to which religion has never opposed anything but unreal and ineffectual barriers; ignorance and servitude make men wicked and unhappy. Science, reason and liberty alone can cure them and make them happier; but everything conspires to blind them and to confirm them in their bewilderment; priests deceive them, tyrants corrupt the better to enslave them; tyranny has been and always will be the real source both of the depravity of behaviour and the habitual calamities of peoples; the latter, almost always bewitched by their religious notions or their metaphysical fancies, rather than casting their eyes on the natural and visible causes of their miseries, attribute their vices to the imperfection of their nature and their misfortunes to the anger of the gods. They offer vows, sacrifices and gifts to heaven in order to win an end to their sorrows which are due only to the negligence, ignorance and perversity of their guides, to the folly of their institutions, to their mad customs, to their false opinions, to their barely rational laws, and above all to their lack of enlightenment. Let minds be filled in good time with true ideas, let men's reason be nurtured, let justice govern them, and there will be no need to oppose the helpless barrier of fear of the gods to the passions. Men will be good when they are well instructed, well governed, punished or despised for doing evil and justly recompensed for their good towards their fellow citizens.

It is vain to pretend to cure men of their vices if a start has not been made in curing their prejudices. It is only by being shown the truth that they will recognize their most cherished interests and the real motives that should lead them to the good. For long enough, the people's instructors have fixed their eyes on the sky: let them at last bring them back to earth. Worn out by an inconceivable theology, ridiculous fables, impenetrable mysteries, puerile ceremonies, let the human mind concern itself with natural things, intelligible subjects, tangible truths and useful knowledge. Once the vain fancies that obsess peoples are dissipated, soon rational opinions will come of themselves to win those human minds which have always been thought to be destined for error.

VII

The Political Solution

The revolutionary potential of Enlightenment thought lay in its emphasis on environment as the formative influence in shaping human nature and on the social origins of evil. From this complex of ideas was born the faith in political reconstruction.

So often has the word enlightened been attached to eighteenth-century despotism that it is commonly assumed that Enlightenment thinkers were ardent monarchists. This might be true of Voltaire in some of his moods, but as a generalization it makes the political thought of the time more authoritarian and much more systematic than it actually was. On the whole, the age was more concerned about the uses to which power was put than the hands in which it was placed. This at any rate was the case of the political ideas of the *Encyclopédie*. In his articles 'Autorité politique', 'Liberté naturelle' and 'Liberté civile', de Jaucourt, who wrote many of the political articles, did little more than paraphrase Locke and Montesquieu. Legitimate political authority must derive from the consent of the people and cannot be created by mere force or violence. Popular consent is given in a contract, real or assumed, by which citizens renounce some of their powers outside civil society whilst rulers pledge themselves to abide by certain conditions. This limitation of government is defined by natural law or natural rights which it cannot be assumed men would repudiate willingly. Within society, men should not be subject to the arbitrary will of individuals, but only to regulation by general and known laws; and the best way of ensuring this is by the separation of the legislative and executive powers.

These ideas were radical enough when placed in the context of French society and government, but there was little that was original in them. They were liberal rather than democratic, aimed at determining the extent rather than the locus of power. With Rousseau, the emphasis shifts. Using traditional contractual language, he ends with a justification of popular rule. His object was to create a society in which

63

men are free, not just in the sense that they have a considerable area of action beyond state interference or in the sense that they are governed only by laws, but because the social rules to which they are subject are accepted by each of them individually, are self-prescribed. The means to this end is the retention of sovereignty by the whole community. If each man concurs in the general will and if the general will legislates, the conditions of true freedom are present. The emphasis thus shifts with Rousseau. How far it shifts is a matter of dispute. Rousseau has been seen as an originator in many areas of thought and sensibility, as an anti-*philosophe* as well as a *philosophe*. In politics, he has been painted as both an advocate of a well-nigh anarchist individualism and an influential precursor of totalitarian ideas (see Gierke, p. 168, for a modified expression of the first view and Talmon, p. 111, for an unqualified statement of the second). Whichever interpretation is correct (if either is correct) and whatever the novelty of Rousseau's writings, any portrait of him that ignores his liberal aspirations or neglects the democratic strain within Enlightenment thought as a whole is bound to be distorted.

With Bentham we come firmly back to a central theme of the age. We have seen how the pursuit of happiness was taken to be the key to the mysteries of human psychology. Men do seek to avoid pain and promote their pleasure and, in doing so, they have become aware of their dependence on others and of the equal claims of others to happiness. Thus the moral feelings are born. But, to use Bentham's phrase, it is for pleasure and pain 'to point out what we ought to do, as well as to determine what we shall do'. The happiness principle is therefore also a standard of right action. In the hands of Helvétius, Beccaria and above all Bentham, the principle was further extended from a moral criterion to a criterion of legislation. The legislator too should be concerned with happiness or utility. In the rules he lays down and the punishments he imposes, he should always aim at a favourable balance of pleasure over pain. This theory left a number of unanswered questions. What *was* the criterion of right behaviour—the happiness of the individual or the general utility? And if the two coincided (as it was thought they did in the economic sphere), what need was there for legislative rules? Was the greatest happiness of the greatest number equivalent to the greatest happiness of the majority? Whatever the ambiguities of the theory, much was expected of it and it proved in fact to be a powerful lever of reform, particularly in the field of penal law. Bentham did not become a democrat until late in his life, after the turn of the century. He then tried to give a utilitarian defence of universal suffrage, but earlier, far from thinking that democracy was entailed by the utility principle, he had called the Rousseauist notions of the general will and the sovereignty of the people 'nonsense on stilts'.

There is no one set of ideas that can be isolated as the political theory of the Enlightenment, although a movement that embraced Locke, Montesquieu, Rousseau and Bentham can hardly be said to be lacking in political theories. What unites these thinkers, what has so often been taken in praise or blame to be their central characteristic, is the developing hope that political solutions could be found for ills that others had seen as endemic in the human condition.

24 Political Theory of the *Encyclopédie*

From the article 'Autorité politique'

No man has received from nature the right to rule others. Liberty is a gift of heaven and each individual of the same species has the right to enjoy it as soon as he enjoys reason. If nature has established any authority, it is paternal power, but paternal power has its limits, and in the state of nature it would end as soon as children were in a position of self-dependence. All other authority originates in something other than nature. Close examination will show that it derives from one of two sources, either the force and violence of those who take possession of it, or the consent of those who have submitted to it through a contract made or assumed between them and whoever they have vested with authority.

Power acquired by violence is nothing but usurpation and lasts only as long as the strength of the ruler prevails over that of the ruled; so that, if the latter become the strongest in their turn and shake off the yoke, they do this with as much right and justice as the other when he imposed on them. The same law which created authority then destroys it: this is the law of the strongest.

Sometimes the authority that has been established by violence changes its nature; this is when it continues and holds together by the express consent of those who have been submitted to it; but through this it enters into the second category, of which I am about to speak, and he to whom it has been granted ceases to be a tyrant and becomes a prince.

Power derived from popular consent necessarily implies conditions that make its exercise legitimate, useful to society and advantageous to the republic, and that fixes and restrains it within certain limits; for a man neither should nor can alienate himself wholly and unreservedly to another man, since he has a master superior to all, to whom he belongs in his entirety. . . .

The prince derives from his subjects the authority he holds over them, and this authority is limited by the laws of nature and of the state. The laws of nature and of the state are the conditions under which they have or are supposed to have submitted themselves to his rule. One of these conditions is that, having no power or authority over them except by their choice and consent, he can never use this authority to break the act or contract by which it has been conferred on him; from then on, he would be acting against himself, since his authority can continue to exist only through the title that has established it. Whoever annuls one destroys the other. Thus the prince cannot dispose of his power and of his subjects without the consent of the nation or independently of the choice laid down in the contract of submission. If he makes other use of it, everything is null and the law will deprive him of the promises and oaths he could make, like a minor who has acted in ignorance, since he is claiming to dispose of what he has only on trust and under entail as if he held it unconditionally and in full ownership.

From the article 'Liberté naturelle'

The right that nature gives to all men to dispose of their persons and their property in the way they judge most conducive to their happiness, under the restriction that they do so within the terms of natural law and that they do not misuse it to the detriment of other men. Natural laws are therefore the rule and the measure of this liberty, for, although men in the primitive state of nature are independent one towards another, they are all dependent on natural laws, by which they should direct their actions.

The first state that man acquires by nature and that is esteemed the most precious of all his possible possessions is the state of liberty. He can neither exchange himself for another, nor sell himself, nor be enslaved, for all men are naturally born free, that is to say they are not subject to the power of a master and no-one has a right of ownership over them.

By virtue of this state, all men hold from nature itself the power to do what seems right to them and to regulate their actions and their property at will, provided they do not act against the laws of the government to which they have subjected themselves.

From the article 'Liberté civile'

This is natural liberty stripped of that part which formed the independence of individuals and the community of goods, so that men might live under laws which gain security and liberty for them. This civil liberty consists at the same time in not having to do anything that the law does not lay down, and men are only in this position because they are governed by civil laws. Thus the better the laws, the happier is liberty.

As Montesquieu has said, no word has presented itself to the mind in so many different guises as liberty. Some have taken it to be the ability to depose those to whom they have given a tyrannical power; others to be the ability to elect those whom they must obey; some have taken this word to mean the right to be armed and to be able to exercise force, and others the privilege of being governed only by a man of their own nation or by their own laws. Several have attached the name to a particular form of government and have denied it to other forms. Those who have experienced republican government have given it to this government, whilst those who have enjoyed monarchical government have given it to monarchy. Indeed each has called liberty living under a government that answers to his customs and inclinations; but liberty is the right to do what the laws permit, and, if a citizen could do what they forbid, he would no longer have liberty, for others would all have likewise this power. It is true that this liberty is found only in moderate governments, that is to say governments whose constitution is such that no-one is forced to do those things the law does not oblige and prevented from doing those the law allows. . . . In consequence, there is no liberty in states when the legislative and executive powers are in the same hands. For greater reason, there is no liberty in those in which judicial power is united with legislative and executive power.

25 Rousseau and Democracy

Jean-Jacques Rousseau (1712–78) was born in Geneva of Protestant parents. His mother died immediately after his birth and his father abandoned him at the age of ten. After an unsettled childhood and early manhood, he arrived in Paris at the age of thirty. He did not make his mark until in 1749 he won a prize offered by the Academy of Dijon with his Discours sur les sciences et les arts. *This reputation was cemented by the* Discours sur l'inégalité *(1755),* La nouvelle héloïse *(1760), the* Contrat social *(1762) and* Émile *(1762). His suspicious, paranoic nature, coupled with experience of real persecution, brought him into conflict with even those intellectuals who befriended him, such as Diderot and Hume. In all his writings, beneath paradox and ambiguity, there is an original genius at work. This originality often led him to ideas foreign to most other* philosophes *and has prompted the portrait of him as an anti-*philosophe *and a father of Romanticism. Such a bald judgment misses the tensions within Enlightenment thought and the degree to which the problems that racked Rousseau were felt by others.*

From *Contrat social*

'The problem is to find a form of association which will defend and protect with the whole common force the person and goods of each associate, and in which each, while uniting himself with all, may still obey himself alone, and remain as free as before.' This is the fundamental problem of which the *Social Contract* provides the solution.

The clauses of this contract are so determined by the nature of the act that the slightest modification would make them vain and ineffective; so that, although they have perhaps never been formally set forth, they are everywhere the same and everywhere tacitly admitted and recognized, until, on the violation of the social compact, each regains his original rights and resumes his natural liberty, while losing the conventional liberty in favour of which he renounced it.

These clauses, properly understood, may be reduced to one—the total alienation of each associate, together with all his rights, to the whole community; for, in the first place, as each gives himself absolutely, the conditions are the same for all; and, this being so, no one has any interest in making them burdensome to others.

Moreover, the alienation being without reserve, the union is as perfect as it can be, and no associate has anything more to demand: for, if the individuals retained certain rights, as there would be no common superior to decide between them and the public, each, being on one point his own judge, would ask to be so on all; the state of nature would thus continue, and the association would necessarily become inoperative or tyrannical.

Finally, each man, in giving himself to all, gives himself to nobody;

and as there is no associate over which he does not acquire the same right as he yields others over himself, he gains an equivalent for everything he loses, and an increase of force for the preservation of what he has.

26 Bentham and Utility

Jeremy Bentham (1748–1832) seems to belong to the nineteenth century more than to the eighteenth, for it was then that his writings had their major effect in the legal, constitutional and economic fields. Nevertheless, he was a true child of the Enlightenment, developing the ideas of previous writers such as Helvétius, Hutcheson and Beccaria. He was born in London, the son of an attorney, and was educated at Oxford, where he took his degree at the tender age of fifteen. Although he was called to the Bar, he never practised law but devoted his life to writing. The Introduction to the Principles of Morals and Legislation *was published in 1789.*

From *An Introduction to the Principles of Morals and Legislation*

1.   NATURE has placed mankind under the governance of two sovereign masters, *pain* and *pleasure*. It is for them alone to point out what we ought to do, as well as to determine what we shall do. On the one hand the standard of right and wrong, on the other the chain of causes and effects, are fastened to their throne. They govern us in all we do, in all we say, in all we think: every effort we can make to throw off our subjection, will serve but to demonstrate and confirm it. In words a man may pretend to abjure their empire: but in reality he will remain subject to it all the while. The *principle of utility* recognizes this subjection, and assumes it for the foundation of that system, the object of which is to rear the fabric of felicity by the hands of reason and of law. Systems which attempt to question it, deal in sounds instead of senses, in caprice instead of reason, in darkness instead of light.

But enough of metaphor and declamation: it is not by such means that moral science is to be improved.

2.   The principle of utility is the foundation of the present work: it will be proper therefore at the outset to give an explicit and determinate account of what is meant by it. By the principle of utility is meant that

principle which approves or disapproves of every action whatsoever, according to the tendency which it appears to have to augment or diminish the happiness of the party whose interest is in question: or, what is the same thing in other words, to promote or to oppose that happiness. I say of every action whatsoever; and therefore not only of every action of a private individual, but of every measure of government.

3. By utility is meant that property in any object, whereby it tends to produce benefit, advantage, pleasure, good, or happiness, (all this in the present case comes to the same thing) or (what comes again to the same thing) to prevent the happening of mischief, pain, evil, or unhappiness to the party whose interest is considered: if that party be the community in general, then the happiness of the community: if a particular individual, then the happiness of that individual.

4. The interest of the community is one of the most general expressions that can occur in the phraseology of morals: no wonder that the meaning of it is often lost. When it has a meaning, it is this. The community is a fictitious *body*, composed of the individual persons who are considered as constituting as it were its *members*. The interest of the community then is, what?—the sum of the interests of the several members who compose it.

5. It is in vain to talk of the interest of the community, without understanding what is the interest of the individual. A thing is said to promote the interest, or to be *for* the interest, of an individual, when it tends to add to the sum total of his pleasures: or, what comes to the same thing, to diminish the sum total of his pains.

6. An action then may be said to be conformable to the principle of utility, or, for shortness sake, to utility, (meaning with respect to the community at large) when the tendency it has to augment the happiness of the community is greater than any it has to diminish it.

7. A measure of government (which is but a particular kind of action, performed by a particular person or persons) may be said to be conformable to or dictated by the principle of utility, when in like manner the tendency which it has to augment the happiness of the community is greater than any which it has to diminish it.

VIII

Progress and History

No idea is more consistently associated with the Enlightenment than that of progress. Yet the idea was not clearly formulated until late in the century and recent scholarship has traced a strong strain of historical pessimism in the thought of the *philosophes* (see Vyverburg, p. 185).

Nevertheless the articulated theory urged by Turgot and Condorcet grew out of many of the commonest assumptions of the time. Men are shaped by environment and it is nurture not nature that corrupts them —these rooted beliefs inspired the hope that by education and political action men could consciously and wilfully mould their world and therefore themselves; and hopes often merged into expectations. Yet more central to the developed theory of progress was veneration of the scientific method. Both Turgot and Condorcet rest their faith in the future on the assumption that an advance in knowledge is firmly assured. The inevitability of progress was an integral part of the empirical scientific outlook. As the body of experiment and observation grew, as hypotheses were tested and refined, as one generation built on the findings of previous generations, the structure of scientific knowledge would rise and be perfected. Progressive enlightenment, in the sense of the growth of the sum of knowledge, was thus guaranteed by the scientific method itself. Condorcet at least assumed that progressive enlightenment, in the sense of the gradual diffusion of knowledge, was equally assured. Here again, he simply extends the logic of previous assumptions. For all the many works of popular science, and especially the *Encyclopédie* itself, were far less attempts to add to knowledge than expressions of confidence in the possibility and utility of increasing the number of the knowledgeable.

What strikes a jarring note on the modern ear is not the belief in the necessary advance of science—for who would now have the temerity to dispute this article of faith? It is rather the steady anticipation of moral progress. What, we might ask, are the means by which moral positions can be demonstrated as universally valid? And what can be meant by progress in morality? These questions have their roots of course in the eighteenth century itself, in Hume's dissociation of reason and morality. But Hume's position was far from being generally accepted or even commonly understood. For most, the true principles of morality were discernible through reason and could therefore, like our knowledge of the natural world or of society, be ever more fully understood and ever more widely appreciated.

This hopeful creed depended on the expectation of greater human powers; it rested also on the knowledge of past achievements. Irritation with the confused, haphazard, accidental, vacillating nature of human development could turn Enlightenment thinkers away from man's actual history towards 'natural' history, the sketch of the logical development of human faculties. But the idea of progress could and did give a guide line in the writing of empirical history. Philosophic or universal history was the ideal as against mere chronicle, for it was only when the historian rose above the accidents and the minutiae of simple narrative that he could trace the emergence of reasonable man. It is this ambition, this confidence in the progressive movement of history and the concomitant conviction of the backward, irrational nature of past societies, that has precipitated charges such as Coleridge's 'ignorant contempt for antiquity'. The quotation from Voltaire shows, at any rate, that the disdain for chronicles and the demand that history be written for the citizen and the philosopher could fertilize a rich crop of historical questions.

27 Turgot and the Fact of Progress

Anne Robert Jacques Turgot (1727–81) was born in Normandy and, like so many other philosophes, was intended for the Church. In the event, he became an administrator and, of all the philosophes, had the most extensive political experience. He was for a time comptroller-general of finance under Louis XVI and tried to reform the fiscal system. He was one of the leading Physiocrats, the group of economic writers who developed laissez-faire theories.

From *Discours aux Sorboniques, le 11 décembre 1750*

The phenomena of nature, submitted to constant laws, are enclosed within an ever recurring cycle; everything is reborn, everything perishes; and, in the successive generations by which plants and animals reproduce themselves, at each instant time only renews the image of what it has wiped away.

The succession of men, on the other hand, shows from age to age a continually varying sight. Reason, the passions, liberty constantly give rise to new events: all the generations are linked to one another by a series of causes and effects which links the present condition of the world with all those that have preceded it. The arbitrary symbols of speech and writing, by giving men the means of securing their hold on their ideas and of communicating them to others, have built up from all the individual pieces of knowledge a common treasure which one generation transmits to the next, as a heritage continually augmented by the discoveries of each age; and the whole human species, looked at from its origins, seems in the eyes of the philosopher, an immense whole which has itself, like each individual, its infancy and its progress.

One can see the establishment of societies and the formation of nations, which dominate turn by turn and bow down to other nations; empires rise and fall; laws and forms of government succeed one another; the arts and sciences are turn by turn opened up and perfect themselves; turn by turn slowed down and accelerated in their progress, they move from region to region; interest, ambition, vainglory change the face of the world at every moment, swamp the earth with blood; yet amidst their ravages, customs and behaviour soften, the human mind becomes enlightened, isolated nations draw closer together; finally trade and politics unite the whole globe, and the totality of humanity, fluctuating between calm and agitation, good times and bad, moves steadily though slowly towards a greater perfection.

28 Condorcet and the Hopes for Progress

Antoine Nicolas Condorcet (1743–94) was born in St Quentin, the son of an army officer. Of aristocratic parents and brought up by clerics, he became an ardent sceptic and an enemy of all privilege. He rose to eminence as a mathematician, but, when the Revolution broke out, he took an active political role, siding usually with the Girondins. He was forced into hiding by the Jacobins, was discovered and died in jail. It was whilst he was in hiding that he wrote his Progrès de l'esprit humain *(1794).*

From *Esquisse d'un tableau historique des progrès de l'esprit humain*

If man can predict with almost complete confidence the phenomena whose laws he knows; if, even when he is ignorant of these laws, he can, from experience of the past, foresee the events of the future with a high degree of probability; why should it be thought a vain enterprise to trace with some verisimilitude a sketch of the future destiny of the human race from the results of its history? The sole foundation of belief in the natural sciences is this idea that the general laws, known or unknown, which rule the phenomena of the universe are necessary and constant; and why should this principle be less true for the development of the intellectual and moral faculties of man than for the other operations of nature? Finally, since opinions formed from experience of the past on objects of the same order are the only rule of conduct for the wisest man, why should the philosopher be forbidden to rest his conjectures on the same foundation, provided that he does not attribute to them a greater certainty than can be derived from the number, invariability and accuracy of observations?

Our hopes for the future state of humanity can be reduced to three important points: the destruction of inequality between nations; the progress of equality within a single nation; finally, the real perfecting of man. Will all nations one day draw near to the state of civilization reached by the most enlightened, the most free, the least prejudiced nations, such as the French and the Anglo-Americans? Will the immense gap that separates these peoples from the servitude of nations subject to kings, from the barbarism of African tribes, from the ignorance of savages be gradually bridged?

Are there countries on the earth whose inhabitants nature has condemned never to enjoy liberty, never to exercise their reason?

These differences of intelligence, resources or wealth between the different classes making up the community, observable in every civilized nation up to the present; this inequality which the first advances of society have increased and so to speak produced; does this derive from civilization itself or is it due to the present imperfections of social techniques? Will it grow continually weaker to give way to that actual equality, the final end of the social art, which, diminishing even the effects of natural differences in abilities, leaves in existence only an inequality helpful to the interests of all, because it will favour the progress of civilization, of education and of industry without involving either subjection or humiliation or impoverishment? In a word, will

men approach that state in which all will have the understanding necessary to conduct themselves according to their own reason in the
ordinary affairs of life and to keep it free from prejudices, to understand fully their own rights and to exercise them according to their
judgment and conscience; that state in which, by the development of
their faculties, all will be able to obtain sure means of providing for
their needs; in which finally stupidity and misery will no longer be
anything except accidents and not the habitual state of a portion of
society?

Lastly, will the human species improve, either by new discoveries in
the sciences and arts and, by a necessary consequence, in the means of
promoting private welfare and common prosperity; or by progress in
the principles of conduct and in practical morality; or finally by the
real perfecting of the intellectual, moral and physical faculties, which
can be the consequences equally of the perfecting of the instruments
which increase the strength and direct the use of these faculties, or even
of the perfecting of the natural organization of man?

Replying to these three questions, we shall find in the experience of
the past, in the observation of the progress that the sciences and civilization have made up to now, in the analysis of the movement of the
human mind and the development of its faculties, the most powerful
reasons for believing that nature has not set any limit to our hopes.

29 Voltaire and Philosophic History

From *Nouvelles considérations sur l'histoire*

Treaties are put into print, there are descriptions of the pomp of a
coronation, the ceremony of the receiving of a biretta and even of the
entry of an ambassador in which not a porter or a lackey is forgotten. It
is good that there are records of everything so that they can be con-
sulted if need be; and I look on all the big volumes now as dictionaries.
But, having read three or four thousand descriptions of battles and the
terms of some hundreds of treaties, I have found that at bottom I was
scarcely more enlightened. I learnt from them only about events. . . . I
would like to know what the resources of a country were before a war
and if this war augmented or diminished them. Was Spain richer

before the conquest of the New World than today? How much bigger was its population at the time of Charles the Fifth than under Philip IV? Why did Amsterdam contain scarcely twenty thousand souls two hundred years ago? How much larger is the population of England than it was under Henry VIII? Is it true, as it said in the *Lettres persanes*, that there are too few men for the earth and that it is depopulated in comparison with what it was two thousand years ago? . . . Here for a start is one of the objects of the curiosity of whoever wishes to read history as a citizen and as a philosopher. He will be far from restricting himself to this sort of understanding; he will seek out what has been the root vice and the dominant virtue of a nation; why it has been powerful or weak upon the seas; how and to what degree it has added to its wealth over a century; the export registers could tell him this. He will want to know how arts and manufacturing have established themselves; he will follow their movements backwards and forwards from one country to another. Finally, changes in manners and in laws will be his most important objectives. In this way, our knowledge would be of the history of men rather than a small part of the history of kings and courts.

Part Two

THE REACTION TO THE
ENLIGHTENMENT

The Reaction to the Enlightenment

With the outbreak of the French Revolution, Enlightenment thought felt the full force of an assault whose violence stemmed from the passion of men who needed to account for the collapse of their familiar and loved world. In their first bewilderment, the opponents of the Revolution could find no coherent explanation for it and no cogent response to revolutionary ideology. Their immediate reaction was to borrow the myths of the Revolution itself and blame the overturning of their world on conspiracy, the insidious subversion of traditional societies by small, alien groups. At the trial of Cagliostro in Rome, the Bavarian Illuminati were accused of being the malignant sect that had destroyed France and threatened Europe; and, in his *Mémoires pour servir à l'histoire de jacobinisme*, Barruel broadcast the notion that the Revolution was a vast anti-Christian and antimonarchic conspiracy of freethinkers and freemasons. Gradually the counter-revolutionary ideology began to emerge and to clarify these inchoate responses, without abandoning their basic presuppositions. This process of rethinking, in which Burke acted as a catalyst for the whole of European thought, depended on a number of assumptions—that the Revolution was not a simple local phenomenon arising from purely French circumstances, that the revolutionary regime had created an entirely new dimension in politics, the ideological dimension, and that this ideology had been forged by the *philosophes*. This connection of an intellectual movement with a political eruption has remained a central point of controversy amongst historians of both the Enlightenment and the Revolution.

Some of the charges made by the romantics in reaction to the Revolution have also gained a permanent place in the historiography of the Enlightenment. It was on the exaltation of reason that they seized as the principal feature of eighteenth-century thought and the central flaw in revolutionary ideology. Reason had of course meant many different things to the Enlightenment itself and the revolt against reason took on at least as many different and often contradictory forms. The age of reason was attacked both because it presumed to make a science out of

79

politics and because, by ignoring history, it had created a false science; both because it elevated the community at the expense of the individual and because it dissolved all social bonds with its excessive individualism; both because it attacked faith and because it created new faiths. Within these confused strictures, two main lines of criticism can be discerned. To some, like Burke and Guizot, the prime folly of revolutionary ideology was that it wanted too much and too quickly. 'Reason' for them meant the addiction to general theories and formulae in politics and to extravagant hopes of political and moral regeneration; and, they believed, once the addicts gained control, the destructiveness of their policies was matched only by the highmindedness of their declared intentions. The mood here is one of irritation at political ineptitude. Others saw the 'reason' of the hated Enlightenment not simply as a foolish political attitude but as a perverted moral position. Goethe, Coleridge and Carlyle, for example, felt the vital flaw in the 'mechanical philosophy' to be not its utopianism but its barren belief that the calculating reason was a sufficient moral guide. Theirs was an emotional and aesthetic reaction to what they believed was the aridity and sterility of the utilitarian ethic, the full fruit in their eyes of Enlightenment thought. 'Reason' meant for them the faith in the possibility of a rational, self-interested discovery of moral principles. The mood here is one of indignation, even fury, at the blind pride and confident insensitivity, at the impiety and moral inadequacy, of the *philosophes*.

This latter mood is illustrated by the quotations from Goethe, Maistre, Coleridge and Carlyle. The former mood is exemplified in the quotations from Guizot and Tocqueville. Both of these writers were practising politicians, and both picked on the abstractness and impracticality of prerevolutionary thought. They do, however, attempt to trace sociological causes for the structure of Enlightenment thought, and in consequence their criticism of the *philosophes* themselves is more muted. Whilst the *philosophes* are censured for their impatience and lack of realism, the blame is placed finally on a political system that denied them any opportunity of gaining the experience so obviously absent in their ideas. The case of Tocqueville is perhaps the more interesting for, as a liberal, he shared many values with the *philosophes* and never joined wholeheartedly in the fashionable denigration of them. The extent to which liberal views of the Enlightenment were affected in the nineteenth century by the romantic reaction is still better shown by the extract from John Stuart Mill's essay on Coleridge, in which even so apparent an heir of the *philosophes* could castigate them for their negativity and their lack of any historical sense. In Hegel and Engels, yet another view is presented. Much of the romantic characterization is accepted as true, but the Enlightenment is seen as a necessary stage in an inevitable historical development, as a progressive movement in the sense that it prepared the ground for future and yet more worthy historical epochs. For Hegel, world history is the story of the emergence of full freedom, that condition in which men can rationally identify their own purposes with those of the external world. In seeking rational explanations of the natural world, the scientific revolution moved towards a greater realization of freedom; and, in testing traditional social institutions on the anvil of reason, the Enlightenment also made an essential advance. Its social thought and aspirations nevertheless remained abstract and finally destructive, since it posed an ideal rational order as against the real world rather than seeking the rationality inherent in the historical process. Engels too offers the same kind of historicist semi-justification; the philosophy of reason was in fact the ideological superstructure of bourgeois economic interests but it did clear the intellectual ground for modern socialism.

1 Joseph de Maistre

Joseph de Maistre (1753–1821) was born in Savoy and followed his father's path as a legal official. The invasion of Savoy in 1792 by the French Republic disrupted the even tenor of his life. For over two decades he led the uprooted life of the emigré. From 1802 to 1817 he represented the king of Sardinia at Saint Petersburg and there wrote many of the works in which he flayed the Revolution and the philosophy he believed had brought it about.

From *Essai sur le principe générateur des constitutions politiques*

It was not therefore until the first half of the eighteenth century that irreligion really became a force. At once it spread everywhere with incredible speed. From the palace to the cabin, it crept everywhere and infected everything; it followed secret channels and had a hidden but effective action so that the closest observer, although he sees the effects, cannot always discover the causes. By its enormous prestige, it made itself loved even by those of whom it was the deadliest enemy; and the authority which it was about to destroy stupidly embraced it before receiving the deathblow. Soon a simple theory became a formal association, which rapidly graduated into a conspiracy and finally into a great organization covering Europe.

Then for the first time the unique character of eighteenth century atheism revealed itself. It no longer speaks in the cold tone of indifference, still less with the biting irony of scepticism; there is a deadly hatred, a tone of anger and often of fury. The writers of this age, at least the most outstanding, no longer treat Christianity as an inconsequential human error, but hunt it like a mortal enemy: it becomes a fight to the end, a war to the death; and what would seem unbelievable, if we did not have sad proofs of it before our eyes, is that many of these self-styled philosophers raised their hatred of Christianity to a personal hatred of its divine Author. They really detest him as a living enemy is detested. Two men above all, who will be for ever cursed by posterity, have distinguished themselves by a kind of wickedness which might seem beyond the powers of even the most depraved human nature.

However, the whole of Europe having been civilized by Christianity, and its ministers having gained an important place in the politics of every country, civil and religious institutions had been intermingled and even amalgamated to a surprising degree; so that it could be said with more or less truth of every European state what Gibbon said of France, *that this Kingdom had been made by bishops.* It was therefore inevitable that the philosophy of the age did not hesitate to vilify the social institutions identified with the religious principle. This is what happened; every government and institution in Europe displeased it, precisely *because* they were Christian; and *in proportion to* the influence of Christianity, a malaise of opinion, a general discontent seized men's minds. In France especially, this philosophic fury no longer recognized any limits.

From *Soirées de St Pétersbourg*

But do you realize, gentlemen, the source of this flood of insolent doctrines which unceremoniously judge God and call him to account for his orders? They come to us from that great phalanx we call *intellectuals* and whom we have not been able in this age to keep in their place, which is a secondary one. At other times, there were very few intellectuals, and a very small minority of this very small minority were ungodly; today one sees nothing but *intellectuals*; it is a profession, a crowd, a nation; and among them the already unfortunate exception has become the rule. On every side they have usurped a limitless influence, and yet if there is one thing certain in this world, it is to my mind that it is not for science to guide men. Nothing necessary for this is entrusted to science. One would have to be out of one's mind to believe that God has charged the academies with teaching us what he is and what we owe to him. It rests with the prelates, the nobles, the great officers of state to be the depositaries and guardians of the saving truths, to teach nations what is bad and what good, what true and what false in the moral and spiritual order: others have no right to reason on this kind of matter. They have the natural sciences to amuse them, what are they complaining about? As for those who talk or write to deprive a people of a national belief, they should be hung like housebreakers. Rousseau himself agreed with this without dreaming of what he was demanding for himself. What folly it was to grant everyone freedom of speech! This is what has ruined us. The so-called philosophers have all a certain fierce and rebellious pride which does not compromise with anything; they detest without exception every distinction they themselves do not enjoy; they find fault in every authority; they hate anything above them. If they are allowed, they will attack everything, even God, because he is master. See if it is not the same men who have attacked both kings and the God who established them. . . .

2 Johann Wolfgang Goethe

Johann Wolfgang Goethe (1749–1832) published his autobiography, Dichtung und wahrheit, *between 1811 and 1814. In it, emotion is recollected and occasionally reconstructed in tranquillity, but the extract from it powerfully exemplifies the aesthetic reaction to eighteenth-century materialism.*

From *Dichtung und wahrheit*

I remember the 'Système de la nature', which we took a look at out of curiosity. We did not understand how such a book could be dangerous. To us it appeared so grey, so chimerical, so deathlike, that only with difficulty did we endure its presence, and we shuddered before it as though it were a ghost. The author fancies that he specially recommends his work when he assures us in the preface, that he is a decrepit old man just sinking into the grave, and that he wants to announce the truth to his contemporaries and to posterity.

We laughed at him: for we thought that we had noticed that old people really never esteem anything in this world that is lovely and good. 'Old churches have dark windows!—One must ask children and sparrows, what cherries and berries taste like!' Such were some of the maxims with which we joked on every suitable occasion and this is how this book appeared to us: as the very quintessence of senility, tasteless, even in bad taste. Everything was supposed to happen with necessity, and therefore no God. But, so we asked, was it not possible that there might necessarily have to be a God? We admitted, of course, that we could not escape the necessities of day and night, of the seasons, the influence of climate, of physical and animal conditions; but nevertheless we felt that there was something within us which seemed like complete freedom of choice, and again something attempting to balance this freedom.

The hope of becoming more rational, more independent of external things, and indeed, of ourselves, we could not give up. The word 'freedom' sounds so beautiful that we cannot do without it, even though it should denote an error.

Not one of us had read through the book: for we found ourselve deceived in the expectations with which we had opened it. It announced a System of Nature, and we therefore really hoped to learn something about nature, our idol. Physics and chemistry, astronomy and geography, natural history and anatomy, and much else, for year right down to yesterday had pointed to this well-adorned universe; and we should have liked to hear both in detail and in general of suns and stars, of planets and moons, of mountains, valleys, rivers and oceans and of all that lives and moves in them. That in the course of this much could happen that might appear harmful to the vulgar, dangerous to the clergy, inadmissible to the State, of that we had no doubt; and we hoped that this little volume might not unworthily have passed the ordeal of fire. But how hollow and empty we began to feel in this melancholy atheistic twilight, in which the earth disappeared with all its forms, and the heaven with all its stars. This idea of a matter from all eternity, for ever in motion and which was now supposed to produce by means of this motion to the right and left and to all side without anything further, the infinite phenomena of existence! We might even have been satisfied with all this, if the author had really built up the world out of his matter or motion before our eyes. But he seemed to know of nature as little as ourselves: for having laid down some general conceptions, he immediately abandons them in order to change that which appears loftier than nature, or as a higher nature within nature, into a material, heavy nature, which—though in motion —is without direction and form; and in this way he fancies himself to have gained a great deal.

If on the one hand this book did us some damage, because we began to feel a hearty dislike towards all philosophy and especially towards metaphysics; on the other, we threw ourselves with even greater gusto and passion into science, experience, action and poetry, which are alive.

3 Samuel Taylor Coleridge

Samuel Taylor Coleridge (1772–1834) at first reacted with joy to the French Revolution but, after the subsidence of his early radicalism, became one of the most bitter critics of 'French philosophy'. He was an admirer of German ideas and helped to introduce German idealism into England.

From *The Statesman's Manual*

I will turn to a subject on which all men of reflection are at length in agreement—the causes of the revolution and fearful chastisement of France. We have learned to trace them back to the rising importance of the commercial and manufacturing class, and its incompatibility with the old feudal privileges and prescriptions; to the spirit of sensuality and ostentation, which from the court had spread through all the towns and cities of the empire; to the predominance of a presumptuous and irreligious philosophy; to the extreme overrating of the knowledge and power given by the improvements of the arts and sciences, especially those of astronomy, mechanics, and a wonder-working chemistry; to an assumption of prophetic power, and the general conceit that states and governments might be and ought to be constructed as machines, every movement of which might be foreseen and taken into previous calculation; to the consequent multitude of plans and constitutions, of planners and constitution-makers, and the remorseless arrogance with which the authors and proselytes of every new proposal were ready to realize it, be the cost what it might in the established rights, or even in the lives, of men; in short, to restlessness, presumption, sensual indulgence, and the idolatrous reliance on false philosophy in the whole domestic, social, and political life of the stirring and effective part of the community: these all acting at once and together on a mass of materials supplied by the unfeeling extravagance and oppressions of the government, which 'showed no mercy, and very heavily laid its yoke'. Turn then to the chapter from which the last words were cited, and read the following seven verses: and I am deceived if you will not be compelled to admit that the prophet Isaiah revealed the true philosophy of the French Revolution more than two thousand years before it became a sad irrevocable truth of history. . . .

Of the discursive understanding, which forms for itself general notions and terms of classification for the purpose of comparing and arranging phenomena, the characteristic is clearness without depth. It contemplates the unity of things in their limits only, and is consequently a knowledge of superficies without substance. So much so indeed, that it entangles itself in contradictions, in the very effort of comprehending the idea of substance. The completing power which unites clearness with depth, the plenitude of the sense with the comprehensibility of the understanding, is the imagination, impregnated with which the understanding itself becomes intuitive, and a living power. The reason (not the abstract reason, not the reason as the mere organ of science, or as the faculty of scientific principles and schemes a priori; but reason), as the integral spirit of the regenerated man, reason substantiated and vital, 'one only, yet manifold, overseeing all, and going through all understanding; the breath of the power of God, and a pure influence from the glory of the Almighty; which remaining in itself regenerateth all other powers, and in all ages entering into holy souls maketh them friends of God and prophets' (Wisdom of Solomon vii.); this reason without being either the sense, the understanding, or the imagination, contains all three within itself, even as the mind contains its thoughts and is present in and through them all; or as the expression pervades the different features of an intelligent countenance. Each individual must bear witness of it to his own mind, even as he describes life and light: and with the silence of light it describes itself and dwells in us only as far as we dwell in it. It cannot in strict language be called a faculty, much less a personal property, of any human mind! He, with whom it is present, can as little appropriate it, whether totally or by partition, as he can claim ownership in the breathing air, or make an inclosure in the cope of heaven. . . .

O! if as the plant to the orient beam, we would but open out our minds to that holier light, which 'being compared with light is found before it, more beautiful than the sun, and above all the order of stars' (Wisdom of Solomon vii. 29), ungenial, alien, and adverse to our very nature would appear the boastful wisdom which, beginning in France, gradually tampered with the taste and literature of all the most civilized nations of Christendom, seducing the understanding from its natural allegiance, and therewith from all its own lawful claims, titles, and privileges. It was placed as a ward of honour in the courts of faith and reason; but it chose to dwell alone, and became a harlot by the wayside. The commercial spirit, and the ascendancy of the experimental philosophy which took place at the close of the seventeenth century, though both good and beneficial in their own kinds, combined to foster its corruption. Flattered and dazzled by the real or supposed dicoveries which it had made, the more the understanding was enriched, the more did it become debased; till science itself put on a selfish and sensual character, and immediate utility, in exclusive reference to the gratification of the wants and appetites of the animal, the vanities and caprices of the social, and the ambition of the political, man was imposed as the test of all intellectual powers and pursuits. Worth was degraded into a lazy synonym of value; and value was exclusively attached to the interest of the senses. But though the growing alienation and self-sufficiency of the understanding was perceptible at an earlier period, yet it seems to have been about the middle of the last century, under the influence of Voltaire, D'Alembert, Diderot, say generally of the so-called encyclopaedists, and alas! of their crowned proselytes and disciples, Frederick, Joseph, and Catharine, that the human understanding, and this too in its narrowest form, was tempted to throw off all show of reverence to the spiritual and even to the moral powers and impulses of the soul; and, usurping the name of reason, openly joined the banners of Antichrist, at once the pander and the prostitute of sensuality; and whether in the cabinet, laboratory, the dissecting-room, or the brothel, alike busy in the schemes of vice and irreligion. Well and truly might it, thus personified in our fancy, have been addressed in the words of the evangelical prophet, which I have once before quoted: 'Thou hast said, none is my overseer!—thy wisdom and thy knowledge, it hath perverted thee!—and thou hast said in thy heart, I am, and there is none beside me!' (Isaiah xlvii. 10.)

Prurient, bustling, and revolutionary, this French wisdom has never more than grazed the surfaces of knowledge. As political economy, in its zeal for the increase of food, it habitually overlooked the qualities and even the sensations of those that were to feed on it. As ethical philosophy, it recognized no duties which it could not reduce into debtor and creditor accounts on the ledgers of self-love, where no coin was sterling which could not be rendered into agreeable sensations. And even in its height of self-complacency as chemical art, greatly am I deceived if it has not from the very beginning mistaken the products of destruction, *cadavera rerum*, for the elements of composition: and most assuredly it has dearly purchased a few brilliant inventions at the loss of all communion with life and the spirit of nature. As the process, such the result!—a heartless frivolity alternating with a sentimentality as heartless—an ignorant contempt of antiquity—a neglect of moral self-discipline—a deadening of the religious sense, even in the less reflecting forms of natural piety—a scornful reprobation of all consolations and secret refreshings from above—and as the *caput mortuum* of human nature evaporated, a French nature of rapacity, levity, ferocity and presumption.

4 Thomas Carlyle

Thomas Carlyle (1795–1881), the son of a Scottish stonemason, became one of the most eminent Victorian men of letters. Early in life, he was influenced by German literature, especially Goethe, whose work he translated and with whom he corresponded.

From the essay on Voltaire

[Voltaire's age] was an age of discord and division; the approach of a grand crisis in human affairs. Already we discern in it all the elements of the French Revolution; and wonder, so easily do we forget how entangled and hidden the meaning of the present generally is to us, that all men did not foresee the comings-on of that fearful convulsion. On the one hand, a high all-attempting activity of Intellect; the most peremptory spirit of inquiry abroad on every subject; things human and things divine alike cited without misgivings before the same boastful tribunal of so-called Reason, which means here a merely argumentative Logic; the strong in mind excluded from his regular influence in the state, and deeply conscious of that injury. On the other hand, a privileged few, strong in the subjection of the many, yet in itself weak; a piebald, and for most part altogether decrepit battalion of Clergy, of purblind Nobility, or rather of Courtiers, for as yet the Nobility is mostly on the other side: these cannot fight with Logic, and the day of Persecution is well-nigh done. The whole force of law, indeed, is still in their hands; but the far deeper force, which alone gives efficacy to law, is hourly passing from them. Hope animates one side, fear the other; and the battle will be fierce and desperate. For there is wit without wisdom on the part of the self-styled Philosophers; feebleness with exasperation on the part of their opponents; pride enough on all hands, but little magnanimity; perhaps nowhere any pure love of truth, only everywhere the purest, most ardent love of self.

In such a state of things, there lay abundant principles of discord: these two influences hung like fast-gathering electric clouds, as yet on opposite sides of the horizon, but with a malignity of aspect, which boded, whenever they might meet, a sky of fire and blackness, thunderbolts to waste the earth; and the sun and stars, though but for a season, to be blotted out from the heavens. For there is no conducting medium to unite softly these hostile elements; there is no true virtue, no true wisdom, on the one side or on the other. Never perhaps was there an epoch, in the history of the world, when universal corruption called so loudly for reform; and they who undertook that task were men intrinsically so worthless. Not by Gracchi but by Catilines, not by Luthers but by Aretines, was Europe to be renovated. The task has been a long and bloody one; and is still far from done.

5 François Guizot

François Guizot (1787–1874) became professor of history at the University of France in 1812. During the early years of the Restoration, he held a number of official appointments until he was dismissed for his Liberal sympathies in 1821. Forbidden to lecture in 1825, he was restored to his chair in 1828 and delivered his famous lectures on the history of civilization. He was a leading

*during the July Monarchy, becoming Louis-Philippe's chief adviser
After the February Revolution, he devoted himself largely to historical
s.*

From *The History of Civilization in Europe*

I need hardly say that the onward impulse of the human mind, that
free inquiry was the predominating feature, the essential fact of the
eighteenth century. You have already heard much concerning this fact
from this chair; already you have heard that powerful epoch characterized by a philosophical orator, and by that of an eloquent philosopher. I cannot pretend, in the short space of time which remains to
me, to trace all the phases of the great moral revolution which then
accomplished itself. I would, nevertheless, fain not leave you without
calling your attention to some characteristics which have been too little
remarked upon.

The first,—one which strikes me most, and which I have already
mentioned, is the, so to speak, almost complete disappearance of the
government in the course of the eighteenth century, and the appearance
of the human mind as the principal and almost the only actor.

Except in that which is connected with external relations under the
ministry of the duc de Choiseul, and in certain great concessions made
to the general tendency of opinion, for instance, in the American war;
except, I say, in some events of this nature, perhaps there has scarcely
ever been so inactive, apathetic, and inert a government as was the
French government of this period. Instead of the energetic, ambitious
government of Louis XIV, which appeared everywhere, and put itself
at the head of everything, you have a government which laboured only
to hide itself, to keep itself in the background, so weak and com-
promised did it feel itself to be. Activity and ambition had passed over
wholly to the people. It was the nation, which, by its opinion and its
intellectual movement, mingled itself with all things, interfered in all,
and, in short, alone possessed moral authority, which is the only true
authority.

A second characteristic which strikes me, in the condition of the
human mind in the eighteenth century, is the universality of free inquiry. Up to that time, and particularly in the seventeenth century,
free inquiry had been exercised within a limited and partial field; it had
had for its object sometimes religious questions, sometimes religious
and political questions together, but it did not extend its pretensions to

all subjects. In the eighteenth century, on the contrary, the character of free inquiry is universality; religion, politics, pure philosophy, man and society, moral and material nature, all at the same time became the object of study, doubt, and system; ancient sciences were overturned, new sciences were called into existence. The movement extended itself in all directions, although it had emanated from one and the same impulse.

This movement, moreover, had a peculiar character; one which, perhaps, is not to be met elsewhere in the history of the world: it was purely speculative. Up to that time, in all great human revolutions, action had commingled itself with speculation. Thus, in the sixteenth century, the religious revolution began with ideas, with purely intellectual discussions, but it very soon terminated in events. The heads of intellectual parties soon became the heads of political parties; the realities of life were mixed with the labour of the understanding. Thus, too, it happened in the seventeenth century, in the English revolution. But in France, in the eighteenth century, you find the human spirit exercising itself upon all things, upon ideas which, connecting themselves with the real interests of life, seemed calculated to have the most prompt and powerful influence upon facts. Nevertheless, the leaders and actors of these great discussions remained strangers to all species of practical activity—mere spectators, who observed, judged, and spoke, without ever interfering in events. At no other time has the government of facts, of external realities, been so completely distinct from the government of minds. The separation of the spiritual and temporal orders was never completely real in Europe until the eighteenth century. For the first time, perhaps, the spiritual order developed itself wholly apart from the temporal order: an important fact, and one which exercised a prodigious influence upon the course of events. It gave to the ideas of the time a singular character of ambition and inexperience; never before had philosophy aspired so strongly to rule the world, never had philosophy been so little acquainted with the world. It became obvious that a day must arrive for coming to facts; for the intellectual movement to pass into external events; and as they had been totally separated, their meeting was the more difficult, the shock far more violent.

How can we now be surprised with another character of the condition of the human mind at this epoch, I mean its prodigious boldness? Up to that time its greatest activity had always been confined by certain barriers; the mind of man had always existed amidst facts, whereof some inspired it with caution, and, to a certain extent, checked its movements. In the eighteenth century, I should be at a loss to say what external facts the human mind respected, or what external facts exercised any empire over it: it hated or despised the entire social state. It concluded, therefore, that it was called upon to reform all things; it came to consider itself a sort of creator; institutions, opinions, manners, society, and man himself, all seemed to require reform, and human reason charged itself with the enterprise. What audacity equal to this had ever before been imagined by it!

6 Alexis de Tocqueville

Alexis de Tocqueville (1805–59) is best known for his books De la démocratie en Amérique *and* L'ancien régime, *but he was also an active politician, sitting in the Chamber of Deputies from 1839 to 1848 and serving as vice-president of the Legislative Assembly and Minister of Foreign Affairs during the Second Republic.*

From *L'ancien régime*

France for a long time past had been the most literary amongst all the nations of Europe. Nevertheless, the men of letters had never shown the powers of mind which they displayed towards the middle of the eighteenth century, nor occupied the place which they then took. The like had never been seen amongst us, nor, I think, anywhere else.

They did not take part daily in public affairs as in England; on the contrary they had never lived further away from them; they were not clothed with any authority whatsoever, and filled no public function in a society already full of functionaries.

They did not, however, remain, like most of their fellows in Germany, entirely strangers to politics, withdrawn to the domain of pure philosophy and fine letters. They were constantly occupied with matters that had reference to government. To speak the truth it was their special interest. They were heard every day discoursing on the origin of societies, and on their primitive forms, on the original rights of citizens and on the rights of authority, on the natural and artificial relations of men to each other, on the wrong or the rightfulness of custom, on the very principles of the laws. Penetrating thus every day to the basis of contemporary society, they examined with curiosity its structure and criticized its general plan. All of them, it is true, did not make these great problems the object of a special and profound study; most of them only touched them casually, and, as it were, playfully, but all had to do with them. This kind of abstract and literary politics was spread unequally over all the works of that period, and there was none, from the heavy treatise to the light song, that did not contain a dose of it.

As to the political systems of these writers they varied from one another to such an extent that the man, who tried to harmonize them and form from them a single theory of government, would never get to the end of such a work.

Nevertheless, if we neglect details to arrive at the prime ideas, we easily discover that the authors of these different systems agreed at least in one very general idea, which each of them seems to have equally conceived, which appears to have existed in their minds prior to all their peculiar ideas and to have been their common source.

However far they may have separated in the rest of their course, they all had this single point of departure; they all thought it would be good to substitute simple and elementary rules drawn from reason and natural law for the complicated and traditional customs, which ruled the society of their time.

A good look will show that what may be called the political philosophy of the eighteenth century consisted properly speaking in this one idea. Such an idea was not new; constantly for 3,000 years it had crossed and recrossed the imagination of men without taking root. How was it that it came to take possession this time of the minds of all the writers? Why was it that instead of stopping, as it had often formerly done, in the heads of certain philosophers, it descended to the crowd and took the consistency and heat of a political passion, in such wise that general and abstract theories on the nature of society became the subject of daily conversation amongst those who had nothing to do, and inflamed the imagination even of women and peasants? Why was it that men of letters, who possessed neither rank, nor honours, nor riches, nor responsibility, nor power, became in fact the chief and even the sole politicians of the age, since, while others did the actual work of government, they alone had the authority? I would like in a few words to indicate what an extraordinary and terrible influence these facts, which at first sight only belong to the history of our literature, had on the Revolution and have even to our own days.

It was not by mere chance that the philosophers of the eighteenth century had as a body conceived notions so contrary to those, which in their days still served as the basis of society; these ideas had been naturally suggested to them by the sight of that very society which they all had before their eyes. The spectacle of so many wrongful and absurd privileges, of which the weight was felt more and more, and the cause was less and less understood, drove or rather precipitated the minds of them all simultaneously towards the idea of the natural equality of conditions. Seeing so many irregular and bizarre institutions, the offspring of another age, which no one had attempted to harmonize with each other or to adapt to new needs, and which seemed bound to perpetuate for ever their existence, they readily conceived a loathing for things ancient and for tradition, and they were naturally led to wish to rebuild the society of their age according to a plan entirely new, which each of them traced by the sole light of his reason.

The very position of these writers led them to relish general and abstract theories in the matter of government and to trust them blindly. In the almost unlimited detachment, in which they lived from practice, no experience tempered the ardour of their temper; nothing warned them of the obstacles, which existing facts could put in the way of even the most desirable reforms; they had no idea of the dangers which always accompany the most necessary revolutions. They had not even a presentiment of them, owing to the complete absence of all political liberty the world of practical affairs was not merely badly known, it was quite invisible. In the world of affairs they did nothing, and could not even see what others did in it. They were therefore entirely without that superficial instruction, which the sight of a free society and the sound of its utterances give even to those, who in it have the least share in its government. And so they became much bolder in their novelties, more enamoured of general ideas and of systems, more contemptuous of ancient wisdom, and more confident still in their individual reason, than is generally seen in authors, who write speculative books on politics. The same ignorance gave them the ear and the heart of the crowd. If the French had still taken part, as formerly, in the government in the States-General; if even, they had continued to busy themselves daily in the administration of the country in the provincial assemblies, they would certainly never have let themselves be inflamed, as they then were, by the ideas of the writers; they would have kept a touch on practical business which would have saved them from pure theory.

7 John Stuart Mill

John Stuart Mill (1806–73) was educated by his father, the leading follower of Bentham. Although he never abandoned the utilitarian philosophy in which his father instructed him, he came into contact with Coleridge's ideas in his twenties. He tried to assess the opposite qualities of these two major influences upon him in his essays on Bentham and Coleridge.

From the essay on Coleridge

To insist upon the deficiencies of the continental philosophy of the last century, or, as it is commonly termed, the French philosophy, is almost superfluous. That philosophy is indeed as unpopular in this country as its bitterest enemy could desire. If its faults were as well understood as they are much railed at, criticism might be considered to have finished its work. But that this is not yet the case, the nature of the imputations currently made upon the French philosophers, sufficiently proves; many of these being as inconsistent with a just philosophic comprehension of their system of opinions, as with charity towards the men themselves. It is not true, for example, that any of them denied moral obligation or sought to weaken its force. So far were they from meriting this accusation, that they could not even tolerate the writers who, like Helvétius, ascribed a selfish origin to the feelings of morality, resolving them into a sense of interest. Those writers were as much cried down among the *philosophes* themselves, and what was true and good in them (and there is much that is so) met with as little appreciation, then, as now. The error of the philosophers was rather that they trusted too much to those feelings; believed them to be more deeply rooted in human nature than they are; to be not so dependent, as in fact they are, upon collateral influences. They thought them the natural and spontaneous growth of the human heart; so firmly fixed in it, that they would subsist unimpaired, nay invigorated, when the whole system of opinions and observances with which they were habitually intertwined was violently torn away.

To tear away was, indeed, all that these philosophers, for the most part, aimed at: they had no conception that anything else was needful. At their millennium, superstition, priestcraft, error and prejudice of every kind, were to be annihilated; some of them gradually added that despotism and hereditary privileges must share the same fate; and, this accomplished, they never for a moment suspected, that all the virtues and graces of humanity could fail to flourish, or that when the noxious weeds were once rooted out, the soil would stand in any need of tillage. . . .

Instead of feeling that the effect of a bad social order in sapping the necessary foundations of society itself, is the very worst of its many mischiefs, the philosophers saw only, and saw with joy, that it was sapping its own foundations. In the weakening of all government they saw only the weakening of bad government; and thought they could not better employ themselves than in finishing the task so well begun—in expelling out of every mind the last vestige of belief in that creed on which all the restraining discipline recognized in the education of European countries still rested, and with which in the general mind it was inseparably associated; in unsettling everything which was still considered settled, making men doubtful of the few things of which they still felt certain; and in uprooting what little remained in the people's minds of reverence for anything above them, of respect to any of the limits which custom and prescription had set to the indulgence of each man's fancies or inclinations, or of attachment to any of the things which belonged to them as a nation, and which made them feel their unity as such.

Much of all this was, no doubt, unavoidable, and is not justly matter of blame. When the vices of all constituted authorities, added to natural causes of decay, have eaten the heart out of old institutions and beliefs, while at the same time the growth of knowledge, and the altered circumstances of the age, would have required institutions and creeds different from these even if they had remained uncorrupt, we are far from saying that any degree of wisdom on the part of speculative thinkers could avert the political catastrophes, and the subsequent moral anarchy and unsettledness, which we have witnessed and are witnessing. Still less do we pretend that those principles and influences which we have spoken of as the conditions of the permanent existence of the social union, once lost, can ever be, or should be attempted to be, revived in connexion with the same institutions or the same doctrines as before. When society requires to be rebuilt, there is no use in attempting to rebuild it on the old plan. By the union of the enlarged views and analytic powers of speculative men with the observation and contriving sagacity of men of practice, better institutions and better doctrines must be elaborated; and until this is done we cannot hope for much improvement in our present condition. The effort to do it in the eighteenth century would have been essentially premature, as the attempts of the Economistes (who, of all persons then living, came nearest to it, and who were the first to form the idea of a Social Science), sufficiently testify. The time was not ripe for doing effectually any other work than that of destruction. But the work of the day should have been so performed as not to impede that of the morrow. No one can calculate what struggles, which the cause of improvement has yet to undergo, might have been spared if the philosophers of the eighteenth century had done anything like justice to the Past. Their mistake was that they did not acknowledge the historical value of much which had ceased to be useful, nor saw that institutions and creeds, now effete, had rendered essential services to civilization, and still filled a place in the human mind, and in the arrangements of society, which could not without the utmost peril be left vacant. Their mistake was, that they did not recognize in many of the errors which they assailed, corruptions of important truths, and in many of the institutions most cankered with abuse, necessary elements of civilized society, though in a form and vesture no longer suited to the age; and hence they involved, as far as in them lay, many great truths in a common discredit with the errors which had grown up around them. The philosophers threw away the shell without preserving the kernel; and attempting to new-model society without the binding forces which hold society together, met with such success as might have been anticipated. . . .

The disrespect in which history was held by the *philosophes* is notorious; one of the soberest of them, D'Alembert we believe, was the author of the wish that all record whatever of past events could be blotted out. And indeed the ordinary mode of writing history, and the ordinary mode of drawing lessons from it, were almost sufficient to excuse this contempt. But the *philosophes* saw, as usual, what was not true, not what was. It is no wonder that men who saw, in the greater part of what had been handed down from the past, sheer hindrances to man's attaining a well-being which would otherwise be of easy attainment, should content themselves with a very superficial study of history. But the case was otherwise with those who regarded the maintenance of society at all, and especially its maintenance in a state of progressive advancement, as a very difficult task, actually achieved, in however imperfect a manner, for a number of centuries, against the strongest obstacles. It was natural that they should feel a deep interest in ascertaining how this had been effected; and should be led to inquire both what were the requisites of the permanent existence of the body politic, and what were the conditions which had rendered the preservation of these permanent requisites compatible with perpetual and progressive improvement. And hence that series of great writers and thinkers, from Herder to Michelet, by whom history, which was till then 'a tale told by an idiot, full of sound and fury, signifying nothing', has been made a science of causes and effects; who, by making the facts and events of the past have a meaning and an intelligible place in the gradual evolution of humanity, have at once given history, even to the imagination, an interest like romance, and afforded the only means of predicting and guiding the future, by unfolding the agencies which have produced and still maintain the Present.

8 Georg Wilhelm Friedrich Hegel

Georg Wilhelm Friedrich Hegel (1770–1831) was one of the founders of German Idealism. For the last thirteen years of his life, during which he published most of his important works including the Philosophy of History, *he was professor of philosophy at Berlin.*

From *Philosophy of History*

Thought is the grade to which Spirit has now advanced.[1] It involves the Harmony of Being in its purest essence, challenging the external world to exhibit the same Reason which Subject [the Ego] possesses. Spirit perceives that Nature—the World—must also be an embodiment of Reason, for God created it on principles of Reason. An interest in the contemplation and comprehension of the present world became universal. Nature embodies Universality, inasmuch as it is nothing other than Sorts, Genera, Power, Gravitation, etc., phenomenally presented. Thus *Experimental Science* became the science of the World; for experimental science involves on the one hand the observation of phenomena, on the other hand also the discovery of the Law, the essential being, the hidden force that causes those phenomena—thus reducing the data supplied by observation to their simple principles. Intellectual consciousness was first extricated from that sophistry of thought, which unsettles everything, by *Descartes*. As it was the purely German nations

[1] i.e. in the seventeenth and eighteenth centuries.

98

among whom the principle of *Spirit* first manifested itself, so it was by the Romanic nations that the *abstract idea* (to which the character assigned them above—viz., that of internal schism, more readily conducted them) was first comprehended. Experimental science therefore very soon made its way among them (in common with the Protestant English), but especially among the Italians. It seemed to men as if God had but just created the moon and stars, plants and animals, as if the laws of the universe were now established for the first time; for only then did they feel a real interest in the universe, when they recognized their own Reason in the Reason which pervades it. The human eye became *clear*, perception quick, thought active and interpretative. The discovery of the laws of Nature enabled men to contend against the monstrous superstition of the time, as also against all notions of mighty alien powers which magic alone could conquer. The assertion was even ventured on, and that by Catholics not less than by Protestants, that the External [and Material], with which the Church insisted upon associating superhuman virtue, was external and material, and nothing more—that the Host was simply *dough*, the relics of the Saints mere *bones*. The independent authority of Subjectivity was maintained against belief founded on authority, and the Laws of Nature were recognized as the only bond connecting phenomena with phenomena. Thus all miracles were disallowed: for Nature is a system of known and recognized Laws; Man is at home in it, and that only passes for truth in which he finds himself at home; he is free through the acquaintance he has gained with Nature. Nor was thought less vigorously directed to the Spiritual side of things: Right and [Social] Morality came to be looked upon as having their foundation in the actual present Will of man, whereas formerly it was referred only to the command of God enjoined *ab extra*, written in the Old and New Testament, or appearing in the form of particular Right [as opposed to that based on general principles] in old parchments, as *privilegia*, or in international compacts. What the nations acknowledge as international Right was deduced empirically from observation (as in the work of Grotius); then the source of the existing civil and political law was looked for, after Cicero's fashion, in those instincts of men which Nature has planted in their hearts—*e.g.*, the social instinct; next the principle of security for the person and property of the citizens, and of the advantage of the commonwealth—that which belongs to the class of 'reasons of State'. On these principles private rights were on the one hand despotically contravened, but on the other hand such contravention was the instrument of carrying out the general objects of the State in opposition to mere positive or prescriptive claims. . . .

These general conceptions, deduced from actual and present consciousness—the Laws of Nature and the substance of what is right and good—have received the name of *Reason*. The recognition of the validity of these laws was designated by the term *Eclaircissement* (Aufklärung). From France it passed over into Germany, and created a new world of ideas. The absolute criterion—taking the place of all authority based on religious belief and positive laws of Right (especially political Right)—is the verdict passed by Spirit itself on the character of that which is to be believed or obeyed. After a free investigation in open day, Luther had secured to mankind Spiritual Freedom and the Reconciliation [of the Objective and Subjective] in the concrete: he triumphantly established the position that man's eternal destiny [his spiritual and moral position] must be wrought out *in himself* [cannot be an *opus operatum*, a work performed *for him*]. But the *import* of that which is to take place in him—what truth is to become vital in him, was taken for granted by Luther as something already given, something revealed by religion. *Now*, the principle was set up that this import must be capable of actual investigation—something of which I [in this modern time] can gain an inward conviction—and that to this basis of inward demonstration every dogma must be referred.

This principle of thought makes its appearance in the first instance in a general and abstract form; and is based on the axiom of Contradiction and Identity. The results of thought are thus posited as finite, and the eclaircissement utterly banished and extirpated all that was speculative from things human and divine. Although it is of incalculable importance that the multiform complex of things should be reduced to its simplest conditions, and brought into the form of Universality, yet this still abstract principle does not satisfy the living Spirit, the concrete human soul.

This formally absolute principle brings us to *the last stage in History, our world, our own time.*

9 Friedrich Engels

Friedrich Engels (1820–96) was a close collaborator of Marx, with whom he wrote the Communist Manifesto. Socialism: Utopian and Scientific *was first published in French in 1880, the first English edition appearing in 1892.*

From *Socialism: Utopian and Scientific*

Modern Socialism is, in its essence, the direct product of the recognition, on the one hand, of the class antagonisms existing in the society of today between proprietors and non-proprietors, between capitalists and wage-workers; on the other hand, of the anarchy existing in production. But, in its theoretical form, modern Socialism originally appears ostensibly as a more logical extension of the principles laid down by the great French philosophers of the eighteenth century. Like every new theory, modern Socialism had, at first, to connect itself with the intellectual stock-in-trade ready to its hand, however deeply its roots lay in material economic facts.

The great men, who in France prepared men's minds for the coming revolution, were themselves extreme revolutionists. They recognized no external authority of any kind whatever. Religion, natural science, society, political institutions—everything was subjected to the most unsparing criticism: everything must justify its existence before the judgment-seat of reason or give up existence. Reason became the sole measure of everything. It was the time when, as Hegel says, the world stood upon its head; first in the sense that the human head, and the principles arrived at by its thought, claimed to be the basis of all human action and association; but by and by, also, in the wider sense that the reality which was in contradiction to these principles had, in fact, to be turned upside down. Every form of society and government then existing, every old traditional notion was flung into the lumber-room as irrational; the world had hitherto allowed itself to be led solely by prejudices; everything in the past deserved only pity and contempt. Now, for the first time, appeared the light of day, the kingdom of reason; henceforth superstition, injustice, privilege, oppression, were to be superseded by eternal truth, eternal Right, equality based on Nature and the inalienable rights of man.

We know today that this kingdom of reason was nothing more than the idealized kingdom of the bourgeoisie; that this eternal Right found its realization in bourgeois justice; that this equality reduced itself to bourgeois equality before the law; that bourgeois property was proclaimed as one of the essential rights of man; and that the government of reason, the Contrat Social of Rousseau, came into being, and only could come into being, as a democratic bourgeois republic. The great thinkers of the eighteenth century could, no more than their predecessors, go beyond the limits imposed upon them by their epoch.

Part Three
PROBLEMS OF HISTORIOGRAPHY

I

General Views of the Enlightenment

The patterns of interpretation and the interwoven lines of criticism developed during the early nineteenth century have had modern exponents. Becker published his influential *The Heavenly City of the Eighteenth Century Philosophers* in 1932. In general, his argument seems a reversal of the common view that the Enlightenment was a radical breach with the past and particularly with the Christian tradition. He portrays the *philosophes* as men of faith rather than reason, or better perhaps men with a naïve, unreasonable and even dangerous faith in reason. Believing in a natural law discernible by all and contrasting the potentialities of natural man with the actualities of past and present societies, they postulated an ideal yet achievable order of things which had explosive revolutionary possibilities. In so redefining the Heavenly City in terms of a terrestrial promise and in seeking their reward not in this life but in approval by posterity, they were simply making a secular translation of the language and concepts of that Christianity they attacked so violently. Yet, despite his analogy between medieval and Enlightenment thought, Becker is doing little more than retouching the romantic picture of the *philosophes* as yearners after a futile and destructive ideal.

On the surface, Talmon's thesis seems quite different; for, far from seeing the eighteenth century as a reflection of the thirteenth, he portrays it as a sinister foreshadowing of the twentieth. It was the *philosophes* who first formulated that political and social theory which has been most fully embodied in the totalitarian regimes of the present age. Yet, when Talmon comes to define these totalitarian postulates, his view of the Enlightenment is not far different from that of Becker. In Helvétius, d'Holbach, Rousseau, Morelly and Mably he finds certain common assumptions—the possibility of discerning through reason and realizing through the human will a perfect order of society, the belief not only that men can achieve such an order but also that they inevitably must, and a view of politics that sees it not as governing the periphery of men's lives but as determining their very nature. The final fruition of Enlightenment thought has thus been political Messianism, a system of chiliastic hopes made the more ardent by the infusion into political drives of all the intensity of religious emotion. For Talmon as for Becker, this faith of reason achieved its apotheosis in the French Revolution; and indeed the bulk of his book, *The Origins of Totalitarian Democracy*, is devoted to illustrating how these postulates were developed during the Jacobin dictatorship and the Babeuf conspiracy.

Both of these interpretations of the Enlightenment have been influential, as much perhaps because of their contemporary relevance as because of their historical accuracy. Nevertheless, they have been subjected recently to some criticism. Amongst the critics, none are more direct or pungent than Professors Gay and Cobban.

I The Heavenly City

C. BECKER

I know it is the custom to call the thirteenth century an age of faith, and to contrast it with the eighteenth century, which is thought to be pre-eminently the age of reason. In a sense the distinction is true enough, for the word 'reason', like other words, has many meanings. Since eighteenth-century writers employed reason to discredit Christian dogma, a 'rationalist' in common parlance came to mean an 'unbeliever', one who denied the truth of Christianity. In this sense Voltaire was a rationalist, St Thomas a man of faith. But this use of the word is unfortunate, since it obscures the fact that reason may be employed to support faith as well as to destroy it. There were, certainly, many differences between Voltaire and St Thomas, but the two men had much in common for all that. What they had in common was the profound conviction that their beliefs could be reasonably demonstrated. In a very real sense it may be said of the eighteenth century that it was an age of faith as well as of reason, and of the thirteenth century that it was an age of reason as well as of faith . . .

We are accustomed to think of the eighteenth century as essentially modern in its temper. Certainly, the *Philosophes* themselves made a great point of having renounced the superstition and hocus-pocus of medieval Christian thought, and we have usually been willing to take them at their word. Surely, we say, the eighteenth century was pre-eminently the age of reason, surely the *Philosophes* were a sceptical lot, atheists in effect if not by profession, addicted to science and the scientific method, always out to crush the infamous, valiant defenders of liberty, equality, fraternity, freedom of speech, and what you will. All very true. And yet I think the *Philosophes* were nearer the Middle Ages, less emancipated from the preconceptions of medieval Christian thought, than they quite realized or we have commonly supposed. If we have done them more (or is it less?) than justice in giving them a good modern character, the reason is that they speak a familiar language. We read Voltaire more readily than Dante, and follow an argument by Hume more easily than one by Thomas Aquinas. But I think our appreciation is of the surface more than of the fundamentals of their thought. We agree with them more readily when they are witty and cynical than when they are wholly serious. Their negations rather than their affirmations enable us to treat them as kindred spirits.

But, if we examine the foundations of their faith, we find that at every turn, the *Philosophes* betray their debt to medieval thought without being aware of it. They denounced Christian philosophy, but rather too much, after the manner of those who are but half emancipated from the 'superstitions' they scorn. They had put off the fear of God, but maintained a respectful attitude toward the Deity. They ridiculed the idea that the universe had been created in six days, but still believed it to be a beautifully articulated machine designed by the Supreme Being according to a rational plan as an abiding place for mankind. The Garden of Eden was for them a myth, no doubt, but they looked enviously back to the golden age of Roman virtue, or across the waters to the unspoiled innocence of an Arcadian civilization that flourished in Pennsylvania. They renounced the authority of church and Bible, but exhibited a naïve faith in the authority of nature and reason. They scorned metaphysics, but were proud to be called philosophers. They dismantled heaven, somewhat prematurely it seems, since they retained their faith in the immortality of the soul. They courageously discussed atheism, but not before the servants. They defended toleration valiantly, but could with difficulty tolerate priests. They denied that miracles ever happened, but believed in the perfectibility of the human race. We feel that these Philosophers were at once too credulous and too sceptical. They were the victims of common sense. In spite of their rationalism and their humane sympathies, in spite of their aversion to hocus-pocus and enthusiasm and dim perspectives, in spite of their eager scepticism, their engaging cynicism, their brave youthful blasphemies and talk of hanging the last king in the entrails of the last priest—in spite of all of it, there is more of Christian philosophy in the writings of the *Philosophes* than has yet been dreamt of in our histories.

The Heavenly City of the Eighteenth Century Philosophers (Yale University Press, 1959), pp. 8, 29–31.

2 Becker's Heavenly City

P. GAY

'Before estimating a book it is well to read its title with care,' Becker suggests, and the title of this book briefly states its central theme: the *philosophes* destroyed less well than they knew. They were believers in their most sceptical moods, Christians in their most anti-Christian diatribes . . .

Before launching upon this theme, Becker expounds a general assumption about the relation of change to permanence in history. There is change in history: Thomas Aquinas and David Hume both used the word 'reason' but meant very different things by it, so that to compare their philosophies by investigating simply what they said about 'reason' would do injustice to both. Words persist, but their meanings change. But also there is permanence in history: no era wholly liberates itself from its antecedents, although its spokesmen may proudly (or perhaps anxiously) proclaim that they have made a complete break. Rhetoric may change while ideas persist. Becker suggests that intellectual historians must reckon with this dialectic of permanence and change and must be misled neither by spurious novelty nor by spurious persistence.

This historiographical warning is the most valuable idea in *The Heavenly City*; unfortunately, Becker fails to heed it when he elaborates his thesis. He argues that despite the great change in the climate of opinion between the thirteenth and eighteenth centuries the two centuries were far more closely related than would immediately appear or would be admitted by the *philosophes*. The *philosophes'* claim to be modern must therefore be discounted:

> I know it is the custom to call the thirteenth century an age of faith, and to contrast it with the eighteenth century, which is thought to be pre-eminently an age of reason. . . . In a very real sense it may be said of the eighteenth century that it was an age of faith as well as of reason, and of the thirteenth century that it was an age of reason as well as of faith.

The overriding fault of the *philosophes* was their naïveté: they 'exhibited a naïve faith in the authority of nature and reason'.

This is to fall into the trap of what I have called spurious persistence. It is true that the medieval Catholic rationalists, of whom Thomas Aquinas was the most prominent, assigned to reason an important place in their epistemologies. It is also true—and Becker's reminders are valuable—that the *philosophes* depended upon some unexamined premises which, to the extent that they were unexamined, may be called 'faith'.

But Becker infers far too much from this. Aquinas' rationalism was by no means as characteristic of the thirteenth century as Voltaire's empiricism was of the eighteenth century. Moreover, Becker forgets his own caution that words may be used in many different ways when he argues that 'there were, certainly, many differences between Voltaire and St Thomas, but the two men had much in common for all that. What they had in common was the profound conviction that their beliefs could be reasonably demonstrated'. But the point is precisely that the two philosophers differed over what constitutes reasonable demonstration. For Aquinas reasonable demonstration was deductive and definitional; Voltaire derided such demonstrations as 'metaphysics', as examples of the despised *esprit de système*.

Aquinas and Voltaire both believed that the powers of reason are limited, but they drew sharply different conclusions from this: for Aquinas, that which is inaccessible to human reason concerns the foundations of Christian theology. Where the light of reason does not shine, the lamp of faith supplies illumination. For Voltaire, on the contrary, that which is inaccessible to reason is chimerical. What can never be found ought not to be sought; it is the realm not of the most sacred, but of the most nonsensical—that is, of 'metaphysical' speculation. Where the light of reason does not shine, man must console himself with that philosophical modesty so characteristic of Voltaire's heroes, Newton and Locke. While Aquinas could make categorical statements about the nature of the soul, Voltaire proudly proclaimed his ignorance in such matters. In seeking to show that 'the underlying preconceptions of eighteenth-century thought were still, allowance made for certain important alterations in the bias, essentially the same as those of the thirteenth century', Becker thus unjustifiably plays with the word 'reason'.

Becker plays the same verbal game in his assertion that both centuries were centuries of faith. The word 'faith' usually serves to describe two rather different psychological processes. Thirteenth-century faith (if I may simplify a complex matter) was submission, not necessarily to what was absurd, but to what was beyond proof and, after a certain point, beyond argument. Failure to have faith (as Voltaire put it facetiously) led to burning in this world and in the next. Eighteenth-century faith in reason, while perhaps often naïve, should be designated by the more neutral term 'confidence'. Its affirmations were public, open to examination and refutation. 'Faith in reason' meant simply that for the *philosophes* the method of reason (strictly speaking the scientific method of such natural philosophers as Newton) was superior to other methods of gaining knowledge; it was superior to revelation, authority, tradition, because it was more reliable. In Diderot's pornographic novel, *Les bijoux indiscrets*, there is a charming dream: the dreamer sees himself transported into a building that has no foundations and whose columns rise into the mists. The crowds walking in and around the building are crippled and deformed old men. It is the land of hypothesis, and the cripples are the makers of systems. But there is a vigorous small child, growing into a giant as the dream progresses, who draws near the fantastic building and destroys it with one blow. That giant is Experiment—no dweller of the heavenly city. Did not the *philosophes*, in their reveries, see themselves as that giant? And did they not include thinkers like Aquinas among the lame makers of systems? To denounce the *philosophes* for having faith in reason may be witty, but the paradox solves no problems in intellectual history.

Carl Becker's Heavenly City Revisited, ed. R. O. Rockwood (Cornell University Press, 1958), pp. 29–34.

3 Totalitarian Democracy

J. L. TALMON

This study is an attempt to show that concurrently with the liberal type of democracy there emerged from the same premises in the eighteenth century a trend towards what we propose to call the totalitarian type of democracy. These two currents have existed side by side ever since the eighteenth century. The tension between them has constituted an important chapter in modern history, and has now become the most vital issue of our time. . . .

The essential difference between the two schools of democratic thought as they have evolved is not, as is often alleged, in the affirmation of the value of liberty by one, and its denial by the other. It is in their different attitudes to politics. The liberal approach assumes politics to be a matter of trial and error, and regards political systems as pragmatic contrivances of human ingenuity and spontaneity. It also recognizes a variety of levels of personal and collective endeavour, which are altogether outside the sphere of politics.

The totalitarian democratic school, on the other hand, is based upon the assumption of a sole and exclusive truth in politics. It may be called political Messianism in the sense that it postulates a preordained, harmonious and perfect scheme of things, to which men are irresistibly driven, and at which they are bound to arrive. It recognizes ultimately only one plane of existence, the political. It widens the scope of politics to embrace the whole of human existence. It treats all human thought and action as having social significance, and therefore as falling within the orbit of political action. Its political ideas are not a set of pragmatic precepts or a body of devices applicable to a special branch of human endeavour. They are an integral part of an all-embracing and coherent philosophy. Politics is defined as the art of applying this philosophy to the organization of society, and the final purpose of politics is only achieved when this philosophy reigns supreme over all fields of life. . . .

Enough has been said already to indicate that totalitarian democracy will be treated in these pages as an integral part of the Western tradition. It is vital to add that much of the totalitarian democratic attitude was contained in the original and general eighteenth-century pattern of thought. The branching out of the two types of democracy from the common stem took place only after the common beliefs had been tested in the ordeal of the French Revolution.

From the point of view of this study the most important change that occurred in the eighteenth century was the peculiar state of mind which achieved dominance in the second part of the century. Men were gripped by the idea that the conditions, a product of faith, time and custom, in which they and their forefathers had been living, were unnatural and had all to be replaced by deliberately planned uniform patterns, which would be natural and rational.

This was the result of the decline of the traditional order in Europe: religion lost its intellectual as well as its emotional hold; hierarchical feudalism disintegrated under the impact of social and economic factors; and the older conception of society based on status came to be replaced by the idea of the abstract, individual man.

The rationalist idea substituted social utility for tradition as the main criterion of social institutions and values. It also suggested a form of social determinism, to which men are irresistibly driven, and which they are bound to accept one day. It thus postulated a single valid system, which would come into existence when everything not accounted for by reason and utility had been removed. This idea was, of course, bound to clash with the inveterate irrationality of man's ways, his likings and attachments.

The decline of religious authority implied the liberation of man's conscience, but it also implied something else. Religious ethics had to be speedily replaced by secular, social morality. With the rejection of the Church, and of transcendental justice, the State remained the sole source and sanction of morality. This was a matter of great importance, at a time when politics were considered indistinguishable from ethics.

The decline of the idea of status consequent on the rise of individualism spelt the doom of privilege, but also contained totalitarian potentialities. If, as will be argued in this essay, empiricism is the ally of freedom, and the doctrinaire spirit is the friend of totalitarianism, the idea of man as an abstraction, independent of the historic groups to which he belongs, is likely to become a powerful vehicle of totalitarianism.

These three currents merged into the idea of a homogeneous society, in which men live upon one exclusive plane of existence. There were no longer to be different levels of social life, such as the temporal and the transcendental, or membership of a class and citizenship. The only recognized standard of judgment was to be social utility, as expressed in the idea of the general good, which was spoken of as if it were a visible and tangible objective. The whole of virtue was summed up as conformity to the rationalist, natural pattern. In the past it was possible for the State to regard many things as matters for God and the Church alone. The new State could recognize no such limitations. Formerly, men lived in groups. A man had to belong to some group, and could belong to several at the same time. Now there was to be only one framework for all activity: the nation. The eighteenth century never distinguished clearly between the sphere of personal self-expression and that of social action. The privacy of creative experience and feeling, which is the salt of freedom, was in due course to be swamped by the pressure of the permanently assembled people, vibrating with one collective emotion. The fact that eighteenth-century thinkers were ardent prophets of liberty and the rights of man is so much taken for granted that it scarcely needs to be mentioned. But what must be emphasized is the intense preoccupation of the eighteenth century with the idea of virtue, which was nothing if not conformity to the hoped-for pattern of social harmony. They refused to envisage the conflict between liberty and virtue as inevitable. On the contrary, the inevitable equation of liberty with virtue and reason was the most cherished article of their faith. When the eighteenth-century secular religion came face to face with this conflict, the result was the great schism. Liberal democracy flinched from the spectre of force, and fell back upon the trial-and-error philosophy. Totalitarian Messianism hardened into an exclusive doctrine represented by a vanguard of the enlightened, who justified themselves in the use of coercion against those who refused to be free and virtuous.

The Origins of Totalitarian Democracy (Secker and Warburg, 1952), pp. 1-5.

4 The Talmon Thesis Criticized

A. COBBAN

The thesis which identifies the French Revolution with the triumph of the powers of evil, and attributes this to the influence of the *philosophes*, goes back, of course, as far as Burke and the abbé Barruel. It found its most powerful exponent in Taine. Of the various subsequent attempts to interpret the Enlightenment in these terms only two are of a sufficiently scholarly nature to require attention. The brilliant essay by

Carl Becker on *The Heavenly City of the Eighteenth-century Philosophers* analyses the thought and, by implication, the influence of the Enlightenment. Becker writes: 'I shall attempt to show that the *Philosophes* demolished the Heavenly City of St. Augustine only to rebuild it with more up-to-date materials.' His thesis is that they tried to bring down the Kingdom of God from heaven to earth, to postulate the possibility of mundane perfectibility, to posit an Earthly Paradise within man's grasp. To substantiate their hypotheses, he says, they used the methods of deductive reasoning. This is to identify the Enlightenment with Cartesianism, as indeed Taine also did; and this book will have been written to no purpose if the error of such an interpretation needs to be emphasized. As, however, Becker's thesis has already been subjected to a thorough and to my mind decisive criticism, I will not repeat the arguments against it here.

More recently, another powerful and far-ranging indictment of the thought of the eighteenth century has been produced in *The Origins of Totalitarian Democracy* by Professor J. L. Talmon. His thesis is ingenious and important. Put briefly, it starts with the contemporary judgment that there are two kinds of democracy—empirical liberal and totalitarian Messianic. The latter, which has produced such striking consequences in our own time, originated, he holds, in the thought of the eighteenth century. Its line of development is from eighteenth-century rationalism, by way of social determinism, to belief in a single valid system of society based on faith. The thought of the Enlightenment, Talmon agrees with Becker, amounts in fact to a secular religion; and it has led by an 'inner logic' to political and social Messianism. The theoretical postulates of the eighteenth century, he argues, became political fact in the course of the French Revolution, first in the 'Jacobin improvisation' and then in the 'Babœuvist crystallization'. These are seen as an anticipation of modern totalitarian communism, which is their logical and also their historical sequel. The clue to the understanding of this process, which can be traced in the evolution of practical politics, he finds in the theoretical pattern which unites eighteenth-century enlightened thought with twentieth-century totalitarianism. It may be summed up as the assumption that there is a sole and exclusive truth in politics; it postulates a preordained, harmonious, perfect plan of society; and recognizes only one, all-inclusive sphere of human action, which is the political. According to this doctrine, to summarize Talmon, politics is the art of applying an all-embracing philosophy to the organization of society.

It may be held that this neat bifurcation between liberal and total-itarian democracy is an over-simplification—as Bentham pointed out, total government and total anarchy are both imaginary extremes—but this does not destroy the basic validity of Talmon's analysis of the contemporary situation. What needs to be challenged is not this, but his discussion of totalitarian sources. In the first place, it must be pointed out that the game of chasing origins can easily lead to very peculiar conclusions, as Voltaire indicated when he wrote that all children have parents, but not all possible parents have children. Tracing a line of descent backwards is bound to produce positive results, and then by a simple process of reversion we can create the illusion of a necessary catena of cause and effect. Thus one could trace a train of influence lead-ing from Stalin back through Lenin, Marx, Hegel, Kant, Rousseau, Locke and Hooker to Aquinas. Each link in the chain is valid, yet it must be confessed that, though there are common features and affinities in the ideas of Aquinas and Stalin, the whole has distinctly less value than the parts.

Another possible source of historical error in the study of ideas is an arbitrary and unduly narrow selection of sources, and it may be thought that Professor Talmon has not escaped this danger. He takes his ex-amples of eighteenth-century enlightened thought only from France, and even there excludes most of the major thinkers of the century from his canon. There are only incidental references to Montesquieu and Voltaire, none to the articles in the *Encyclopédie*, none to Turgot, only one to Diderot. The thinkers he relies on, and whom he describes as those who 'do deserve, in our opinion, to be considered as speaking for the eighteenth century', are a very small group, and not all of these are in fact appealed to seriously. Condorcet is mentioned, and his super-ficial sketch of the progress of the human race might seem to make him a profitable candidate for a role in the history of political Messianism. Unfortunately, since he was also the principal author of the 'Girondin' Constitution of 1793, which pushed liberal political ideas beyond the bounds of common sense, he cannot easily be treated as a prophet of totalitarianism, and Professor Talmon makes little use of him. D'Hol-bach was a much more serious political and social thinker, but as has been suggested above, his ideas are profoundly liberal and he also affords little support to the thesis. He is thrown in, occasionally, to make weight with Helvétius, whose crude and immature utilitarianism is indeed sometimes stated in more or less totalitarian terms. However, the strongest support for Talmon's thesis to be found in Helvétius comes in the letters published in 1788, which are now known to be a propaganda publication of that date and falsely attributed to him. Moreover, before allowing that Helvétius is typical of the Enlightenment it would be necessary to take into consideration the severe criticism which Voltaire and Diderot, among others, directed against his ideas.

We are left with three more serious candidates—Morelly, Mably and Rousseau. Morelly's pamphlet, the *Code de la Nature*, has had to bear a weight of argumentation, from both left- and right-wing writers, far beyond what such a slight source can support. Mably's voluminous works are a rag-bag of eighteenth-century ideas. He is capable of expressing the most extreme views, and then limiting and qualifying them in so many ways that they practically lose all significance. He wants to see a free society, but believes that in modern States, and particularly in France, the people are incapable of liberty. Professor Talmon himself truly says of Mably's thought that it is 'entangled in the gravest incongruities and contradictions'. Finally, there is Rousseau, on whom in the last resort the gravamen of the argument rests. The extent to which totalitarian views can be attributed to Rousseau is a much disputed question but one which need not delay us here. Even if one were to agree—which I do not—that Rousseau's political thought is totalitarian, this would only serve to show that he had broken with the liberal, individualist ideas of the Enlightenment, and that the *philosophes* were right in regarding him as their greatest enemy.

There is one last point which must be made. We may agree that Professor Talmon's analysis of the idea of totalitarian democracy is a significant contribution to political thinking; and we may agree with him in deploring the practical consequences of the idea. But such a condemnation requires some standard of values, or some other political system, by comparison with which to make such a judgment. This can only be the alternative system of liberal democracy. Now when we ask where the ideas of liberal democracy come from, we find ourselves thrown back precisely on the Enlightenment, which Talmon has indicted as the *fons et origo* of totalitarianism .... Of course, the same intellectual movement might conceivably be responsible for both liberalism and totalitarianism, but to establish this would require rather more evidence of the supposed totalitarian element in the Enlightenment than we have been given. Before falling back on such an explanation we should see if there is not a less paradoxical one. It would be generally agreed that the turning-point came towards the end of the eighteenth century, and it is consequently reasonable to consider whether we can, or cannot, detect in the Revolutionary and Napoleonic era new trends which may provide a clue to the failure of the high hopes of the Enlightenment, instead of hypothesizing such a basic self-contradiction in its ideas.

In Search of Humanity (Cape, 1960), pp. 181–5.

II

Rationalism

The influence of Cartesian thinking on the Enlightenment is a complex and controversial topic. For some, Cassirer and Cobban for example, the central themes of the age were not affected by Descartes or affected only in a general and indefinite way. Others, such as Vartanian and Frankel, see Cartesian thought as playing a much more vital role. The evidence is by no means clear. Many *philosophes* acknowledged their debt to Descartes, especially as the man who had made the first brave challenge to the intellectual hegemony of tradition and authority. On the other side, most were eager to emphasize their detachment from Cartesianism as a metaphysical system, to claim the title empiricist rather than rationalist, and to attach themselves to the sensationalism of Locke rather than the innate ideas of Descartes. Frankel, seeing the tension between Cartesian rationalism and scientific empiricism as central to the development of eighteenth-century ideas, allows an influence but only a limited influence to Descartes, stressing the importance of his systematic doubt and his analytic method. Vartanian argues that Descartes had a much more direct and specific effect, even on the development of scientific thought. The desire for a universal physics, comprehensive in its scope and completely coherent internally, owed much more to Descartes than to Newton, whose empiricism promised much less grandiose results. Buchdahl, however, claims that Newton offered more than one example and that he too nurtured the ambition to achieve a fully coherent synthesis of physical phenomena expressed in mathematical terms (see pp. 131–4).

5 The *Philosophes* and Descartes

C. FRANKEL

The special position which the *philosophes* gave to Descartes, despite the frequency and vigour with which they attacked his speculative metaphysics, provides a clue to the character of his influence upon them. In general, Descartes' influence on the French Enlightenment did not produce philosophies that announced themselves as Cartesian. It was not to Descartes, but to Francis Bacon, Newton, and Locke that the *philosophes* turned when they looked for exemplars of proper intellectual method. At the same time that the great works in social criticism written during the fifth decade of the century were attacks upon the superstitions of the *ancien régime*, they were also, for the most part, revolts against the Cartesian reinforcement of supernaturalism—the separation of the mind from physical nature. The *philosophes* stressed the fact that they had broken with Cartesianism as a system: Descartes, as Voltaire and others wrote, had discovered the mistakes of antiquity, but he had substituted his own in their place. In following Locke, who had 'reduced metaphysics to what it ought to be in fact, the experimental physics of the soul', the *philosophes* had ceremoniously rejected Descartes' 'metaphysical romance'.

But in the last analysis Descartes seems to have been criticized because, after all, he had not been Cartesian enough. In 1687, Bishop Bossuet had written to a friend that Cartesianism was more than just another heresy, that it was a manifestation of a general spirit of unbelief. If this was Cartesianism, then Descartes, the *philosophes* felt, had not himself been a thoroughgoing Cartesian. For the *philosophes* remembered him as the revolutionary who had made doubting a systematic affair, and as the seer who had revealed the possibility of making mathematics a universal method for all the sciences; consequently, in having separated the mind from the world of measurable things, Descartes could be accused of having failed to carry through the very programme he had initiated. In arguing that there was a substance —*res cogitans*, the mind—to which mathematical method was wholly inappropriate, Descartes had given a metaphysical sanction to the existing social barriers against the extension of free, scientific inquiry into religious, political, and moral domains. That authorities claiming a basis in a super-rational revelation exercised a virtual monopoly of power over social arrangements was something which the *philosophes* recognized to be a fact. But Cartesian metaphysics seemed an attempt to celebrate this recognized matter of fact as an illustration of a necessary and inescapable law. At the very least, Cartesianism had tended to become an elaborate new scholasticism which was a distraction from the important practical business of philosophy; and in certain cases— witness Bishop Bossuet's defence of divine-right absolutism—it had also been used to support the claims of supernatural theology to authority over morals and politics.

So Voltaire could prefer Locke because the Englishman was more Cartesian, more consistently mathematical-minded, than Descartes himself. Descartes had lost himself in speculation, and had surrendered his programme of applying scientific methods to the study of man; but Locke had pushed forward to uncover 'the anatomy of the soul' by placing it within the world of physical bodies in motion. Proceeding from 'well-established facts' and rejecting speculative hypotheses, Locke had nevertheless managed to regain the geometrical manner of analysis, and had shown that, without the smallest assistance from geometry, a man might still possess a truly geometrical intellect.

But if Descartes had not been consistent he had nevertheless set the pattern; and the *philosophes* recognized that Locke and the other luminaries of the Enlightenment were his heirs. When the *philosophes* tried to see themselves in the setting of history, when they tried to connect their programme with its sources, they recognized Descartes as a pivotal figure in the progress of the human mind. Descartes had given the first considerable impetus to the onslaught against the unquestioning acceptance of inherited beliefs. His systematic doubt had dramatized the career of the individual's liberated mind confronting a world that it had never made. 'Until he appeared the study of nature was benumbed, spiritless, and inert. . . . Descartes at least dared to show . . . how to overthrow scholasticism, opinion, authority, in a word, prejudice and barbarism; and through that revolt . . . Philosophy was rendered a service by him.'

Even so relatively conservative a man as Turgot, who stressed the importance to the progress of mankind of Christianity in particular, and of historic continuity in general, recognized the contribution Descartes had made simply as a revolutionary, as a man who had demonstrated the importance and possibility of destroying inherited notions that interfered with the progress of investigation. For the *philosophes* agreed that a new approach to the past was necessary, and the consolidation of this approach they took to be the distinctive achievement of their most philosophic of centuries. In Descartes' conviction that the mind must be purged of the corrupting influence of the past they found a precursor of their own self-conscious 'modernity'.

Furthermore, the specific purge which the *philosophes* used—'the analytic method'—bore a recognized affinity with the method of Descartes. The methodical breaking down of complex ideas into simple, presumably irreducible, sense-impressions displayed, as the Abbé de Condillac observed, . . . the persistence of the mathematical method of

Descartes. Even though the *philosophes* looked upon themselves as 'empiricists' rather than 'rationalists', and thought that the ultimate elements of ideas were sense-impressions rather than self-evident ideas, they shared the basic Cartesian assurance that the human understanding might be solidly reconstructed exclusively out of the simple elements revealed by analysis.

The *philosophes* regarded Descartes, furthermore, as the first great exponent not merely of analysis but of the mechanistic ideal that all nature might be explained in the terms of a universal science of mechanics.

> It was Descartes who . . . made a revolution. The system of occasional causes, the idea of reducing everything to matter and motion, are the main principles of this vigorous philosopher, and imply an analysis of ideas of which the Ancients afforded no example. . . . Locke succeeded in pushing this analysis very much farther. Berkeley and Condillac followed him. They are all children of Descartes.

If the *philosophes* did not agree with each of Descartes' arguments in support of this method of analysis they accepted his metaphysical conclusion concerning the absolute ontological status of that method. The idea of reducing everything to matter and motion was a way of eliminating as 'irrational' or 'unnatural' what could not be so reduced. The *philosophes* sought, as did Descartes, to establish the validity of ideas by showing them to be entirely composed of irreducible simples (albeit clear and distinct 'sensations' rather than clear and distinct ideas) always and everywhere available to men, and to liberate the human mind by purging it of the contingent, the historical, the 'unclear' notions that were the accidents of a particular education in a particular time and place.

Even though the *philosophes* thought they had shifted from 'rationalism' to 'empiricism', their main metaphysical assumption thus remained Cartesian in an important respect. The 'analytic method' of the *philosophes* was not simply a method for investigating the origins of beliefs and ideas. The results it obtained were evaluated in the light of a prepossession about what was ultimate and constant in the universe: the products of analysis—simple sensations—were the invariable ingredients of all experience. Consequently, what was left over and unaccounted for after analysis into simples was temporary, relative, and invalid. It was 'mere' custom, accidental and unreasonable. In terms of this prepossession the analytic method functioned not primarily as a way of investigating the historic development of ideas but rather as a disinfectant intended to rid men of ill-founded or irrational beliefs. Further, the analytic method was the method of *esprits simplistes*. What could not be taken account of by analysis need not be taken account of. The *philosophes* preferred simplicity and took it to be an essential touchstone of validity. The ability to attain solutions that were simple was one of the marks of a good intellectual method and one of the tests of the success of any course of investigation. Not merely must the ultimate elements of ideas be simple, but taken together they ought not to be complicated. Perhaps man cannot know everything. But he may be confident that the problems he can solve require no extraordinary ability, nothing much more than the good sense (which is 'of all things in the world most equally distributed') to see through complications. As Professor Lovejoy has observed, the mental habit of the *esprit simpliste* was one of the more pervasive controlling presumptions of the Enlightenment. It was important precisely because it was so easily and so widely taken for granted. If the *philosophes* joined Locke in the belief that man's knowledge was limited, they also shared his conviction that man could know enough for the purposes of enlightened behaviour, and they agreed with Descartes that what man did know could be easily grasped and simply demonstrated. As Professor Gilson has pointed out, mathematics had been recognized as the most certain science before Descartes, but only Descartes had insisted upon taking it as the exclusive model for all science and denying value to whatever could not attain equal simplicity and certainty. His belief in the universality of the mathematical method was what distinguished Descartes from his predecessors and made him a revolutionary. From the point of view of medieval philosophy he was '*indisciplinatus*', one who 'makes it a point to seek in no matter what discipline a degree of certainty that it does not allow'. It was with this ideal of science, with its 'radical elimination of the probable', that Descartes exerted his fundamental influence on the *philosophes*.

The Faith of Reason (King's Crown Press, Columbia University, 1948), pp. 13–18.

6 Descartes and Physics

A. VARTANIAN

It is a revealing fact that, however much the philosophes repudiated Cartesian physics, they were strangely unable to forget it completely. Their thinking in questions of natural science conformed to a characteristically contrapuntal movement, regulated by the Newton *versus* Descartes theme. It was Fontenelle, perhaps, who had given the original example. His celebrated *Eloge de Newton* had incensed the London Royal Society by daring to draw a parallel between the methodologies of Newton and Descartes on a footing of equality. Fontenelle's early comparison of the two great scientists, skilfully bringing out the diametrical opposition between a deductive-rationalist and an inductive-experimentalist ideal of science, gave the essential content of the Cartesianism that was to persist concurrently with Newtonianism among his younger contemporaries in *lumières* . . . .

The pitting of Newton and Descartes against each other, with varying shades of sympathy being shown for the first or the second, came to be a commonplace device with the philosophes . . . .

The Cartesian standpoint frequently found expression during the Enlightenment as a basis for criticism of Newtonian theories. The latter were blamed for offering at best only a fragmentary, and therefore in all probability a false—or at least undemonstrable—representation of things. One quotation taken from Keranflech's *Hypothèse des petits tourbillons* (written in defence of Cartesian physics at a moment when Newtonianism was everywhere in credit), will serve, as a sample of many similar statements, to illustrate the sense in which Descartes' standard of science survived actively in Diderot's epoch. 'A system of physics is an immense affair,' declared Keranflech. 'It has to do with the general Plan of the Universe; with discovering the arrangement and ordering of its parts, the composition of various bodies, and the mechanism that produces all the effects one observes therein. The problem is to make all these things depend upon a single supposition, a unique principle; to find an idea whose development will be the explanation of the whole of Nature.' Such an affirmation of objectives remained, of course, perfectly consistent with the precedent set by Descartes himself who, at the end of the *Principes de la philosophie*, had asserted that every natural phenomenon was accounted for by his system.

The desirability of a universal physics, as proclaimed by Descartes and his followers, fostered in France a strong faith in the absolute coherence of nature, whose component elements were deemed so completely integrated that no specific phenomenon was to be understood except in relation to the whole. This tendency to view the natural order as a thoroughly interdependent unit complete in itself, and as such to make of it (regardless of whether one accepted or rejected the *tourbillons*) the point of departure for physical inquiry, had, in Diderot's thinking too, an almost axiomatic validity.

Diderot and Descartes (Princeton University Press, 1953), pp. 140–1, 149–50.

III

Empiricism

Since the late eighteenth century, reason has been generally accepted (and usually attacked) as the central characteristic of Enlightenment thought. This is true, for example, of an historian such as Becker, who treats the belief in the constructive and creative possibilities of the human mind with such ironic detachment. For him, the first article in the rationalist credo was that there are certain universal truths which all rational beings are capable of grasping and the perception of which can enable them to reconstruct the conditions of their existence. For Cassirer too reason is the central characteristic of the age, but for him this opaque concept refers to a particular method of thinking rather than the capacity to realize a particular set of truths. This method of thought, new in the eighteenth century, rejected all *a priori* methods and insisted on observation and experiment as the only sure bases of knowledge. The mysteries of the nature of things could only be solved by exact analysis, by referring all hypotheses to empirical data; what was incapable of empirical verification lay outside the bounds of human understanding. Such a method promised, not a leap from ignorance to enlightenment, not sudden riches, but the deliberate and progressive accumulation of knowledge, the gradual acquisition of wealth. This method, in Cassirer's phrase, 'involves recourse to Newton's "Rules of Philosophizing" rather than to Descartes' *Discourse on Method*'. Yet Cassirer sees the Newtonian example as stimulating an effort at synthesis as well as giving an impetus to the analytic method. This idea is developed by Buchdahl, who traces two different images of Newton in the age of reason, the Newton of the *Principia* offering a vast and systematic formula relating phenomena previously believed unconnected, and the Newton of the *Opticks* much less speculative and much more concerned with encouraging the discipline of observation and experiment.

7 L'esprit Systématique

E. CASSIRER

The eighteenth century is imbued with a belief in the unity and immutability of reason. Reason is the same for all thinking subjects, all nations, all epochs, and all cultures. From the changeability of religious creeds, of moral maxims and convictions, of theoretical opinions and judgments, a firm and lasting element can be extracted which is permanent in itself, and which in this identity and permanence expresses the real essence of reason. For us the word 'reason' has long since lost its unequivocal simplicity even if we are in essential agreement with the basic aims of the philosophy of the Enlightenment. We can scarcely use this word any longer without being conscious of its history; and time and again we see how great a change of meaning the term has undergone. This circumstance constantly reminds us how little meaning the terms 'reason' and 'rationalism' still retain, even in the sense of purely historical characteristics. The general concept is vague, and it becomes clear and distinct only when the right 'differentia specifica' is added. Where are we to look for this specific difference in the eighteenth century? If it liked to call itself a 'century of reason', a 'philosophic century', wherein lies the characteristic and distinguishing feature of this designation? In what sense is the word 'philosophy' used here? What are its special tasks, and what means are at its disposal for accomplishing these tasks in order to place the doctrines of the world and of man on a firm foundation?

If we compare the answers of the eighteenth century to these questions with the answers prevailing at the time when that century began its intellectual labours, we arrive at a negative distinction. The seventeenth century had seen the real task of philosophy in the construction of the philosophical 'system'. Truly 'philosophical' knowledge had seemed attainable only when thought, starting from a highest being and from a highest, intuitively grasped certainty, succeeded in spreading the light of this certainty over all derived being and all derived knowledge. This was done by the method of proof and rigorous inference, which added other propositions to the first original certainty and in this way pieced out and linked together the whole chain of possible knowledge. No link of this chain could be removed from the whole; none was explicable by itself. The only real explanation possible consisted in its 'derivation', in the strict, systematic deduction by which any link might be traced back to the source of being and certainty, by which its distance from this source might be determined, and by which the number of intermediate links separating a given link from this source might be specified. The eighteenth century abandons this kind of deduction and proof. It no longer vies with Descartes and Malebranche, with Leibniz and Spinoza for the prize of systematic rigour and completeness. It seeks another concept of truth and philosophy whose function is to extend the boundaries of both and make them more elastic, concrete, and vital. The Enlightenment does not take the ideal of this mode of thinking from the philosophical doctrines of the past; on the contrary, it constructs its ideal according to the model and pattern of contemporary natural science.

The attempt to solve the central problem of philosophic method involves recourse to Newton's 'Rules of Philosophizing' rather than to Descartes' *Discourse on Method*, with the result that philosophy presently takes an entirely new direction. For Newton's method is not that of pure deduction, but that of analysis. He does not begin by setting up certain principles, certain general concepts and axioms, in order, by virtue of abstract inferences, to pave the way to the knowledge of the particular, the 'factual'. Newton's approach moves in just the opposite direction. His phenomena are the data of experience; his principles are the goal of his investigation. If the latter are first according to nature (πρότερον τῇ φύσει), then the former must always be first to us (πρότερον πρός ἡμᾶς). Hence the true method of physics can never consist in proceeding from any arbitrary *a priori* starting-point, from a hypothesis, and in completely developing the logical conclusions implicit in it. For such hypotheses can be invented and modified as desired; logically, anyone of them is as valid as any other. We can progress from this logical indifference to the truth and precision of physical science only by applying the measuring stick elsewhere. A scientific abstraction or 'definition' cannot serve as a really unambiguous starting-point, for such a starting-point can only be obtained from experience and observation. This does not mean that Newton and his disciples and followers saw a cleavage between experience and thinking, that is, between the realm of bare fact and that of pure thought. No such conflicting modes of validity, no such dualism between 'relations of ideas' and 'matters of fact' as we find in Hume's *Enquiry concerning Human Understanding*, is to be found among the Newtonian thinkers. For the goal and basic presupposition of Newtonian research is universal order and law in the material world. Such regularity means that facts as such are not mere matter, they are not a jumble of discrete elements; on the contrary, facts exhibit an all-pervasive form. This form appears in mathematical determinations and in arrangements according to measure and number. But such arrangements cannot be foreseen in the mere concept; they must rather be shown to exist in the facts themselves. The procedure is thus not from concepts and axioms to phenomena, but vice versa. Observation produces the datum of science; the principle and law are the object of the investigation.

This new methodological order characterizes all eighteenth century thought. The value of system, the '*esprit systématique*', is neither underestimated nor neglected; but it is sharply distinguished from the love of system for its own sake, the '*esprit de système*'. The whole theory of knowledge of the eighteenth century strives to confirm this distinction. D'Alembert in his 'Preliminary Discourse' to the French *Encyclopedia* makes this distinction the central point of his argument, and Condillac in his *Treatise on Systems* gives it explicit form and justification. Condillac tries to subject the great systems of the seventeenth century to the test of historical criticism. He tries to show that each of them failed because, instead of sticking to the facts and developing its concepts from them, it raised some individual concept to the status of a dogma. In opposition to the 'spirit of systems' a new alliance is now called for between the 'positive' and the 'rational' spirit. The positive and the rational are never in conflict, but their true synthesis can only be achieved by the right sort of mediation. One should not seek order, law, and 'reason' as a rule that may be grasped and expressed prior to the phenomena, as their *a priori*; one should rather discover such regularity in the phenomena themselves, as the form of their immanent connection. Nor should one attempt to anticipate from the outset such 'reason' in the form of a closed system; one should rather permit this reason to unfold gradually, with ever increasing clarity and perfection, as knowledge of the facts progresses. The new logic that is now sought in the conviction that it is everywhere present on the path of knowledge is neither the logic of the scholastic nor of the purely mathematical concept; it is rather the 'logic of facts'. The mind must abandon itself to the abundance of phenomena and gauge itself constantly by them. For it may be sure that it will not get lost, but that instead it will find here its own real truth and standard. Only in this way can the genuine correlation of subject and object, of truth and reality, be achieved; only so can the correspondence between these concepts, which is the condition of all scientific knowledge, be brought about.

From the actual course of scientific thinking since its revival in modern times the Enlightenment derives its concrete, self-evident proof that this synthesis of the 'positive' and the 'rational' is not a mere postulate, but that the goal set up is attainable and the ideal fully realizable. In the progress of natural science and the various phases it has gone through, the philosophy of the Enlightenment believes it can, as it were, tangibly grasp its ideal. For here it can follow step by step the triumphal march of the modern analytical spirit. It had been this spirit that in the course of barely a century and a half had conquered all reality, and that now seemed finally to have accomplished its great task of reducing the multiplicity of natural phenomena to a single universal rule. And this cosmological formula, as contained in Newton's general law of attraction, was not found by accident, nor as the result of sporadic experimentation; its discovery shows the rigorous application of scientific method. . . .

The philosophy of the eighteenth century takes up this particular case, the methodological pattern of Newton's physics, though it immediately begins to generalize. It is not content to look upon analysis as the great intellectual tool of mathematico-physical knowledge; eighteenth century thought sees analysis rather as the necessary and indispensable instrument of all thinking in general. This view triumphs in the middle of the century. However much individual thinkers and schools differ in their results, they agree in this epistemological premise. Voltaire's *Treatise on Metaphysics*, d'Alembert's *Preliminary Discourse*, and Kant's *Inquiry concerning the Principles of Natural Theology and Morality* all concur on this point. All these works represent the true method of metaphysics as in fundamental agreement with the method which Newton, with such fruitful results, introduced into natural science. Voltaire says that man, if he presumes to see into the life of things and know them as they really are in themselves, immediately becomes aware of the limits of his faculties; he finds himself in the position of a blind man who must judge the nature of colour. But analysis is the staff which a benevolent nature has placed in the blind man's hands. Equipped with this instrument he can feel his way forward among appearances, discovering their sequence and arrangement; and this is all he needs for his intellectual orientation to life and knowledge. 'We must never make hypotheses; we must never say: Let us begin by inventing principles according to which we attempt to explain everything. We should say rather: Let us make an exact analysis of things. . . . When we cannot utilize the compass of mathematics or the torch of experience and physics, it is certain that we cannot take a single step forward.' But provided with such instruments as these, we can and should venture upon the high seas of knowledge. We must, of course, abandon all hope of ever wresting from things their ultimate mystery, of ever penetrating to the absolute being of matter or of the human soul. If, however, we refer to empirical law and order, the 'inner core of nature' proves by no means inaccessible. In this realm we can establish ourselves and proceed in every direction. The power of reason does not consist in enabling us to transcend the empirical world but rather in teaching us to feel at home in it. Here again is evident a characteristic change of meaning in the concept of reason as compared with seventeenth century usage. In the great metaphysical systems of that century—those of Descartes and Malebranche, of Spinoza and Leibniz—reason is the realm of the 'eternal verities', of those truths held in common by the human and the divine mind. What we know through reason, we therefore behold 'in God'. Every act of reason means participation in the divine nature; it gives access to the intelligible world. The eighteenth century takes reason in a different and more modest sense. It is no longer the sum total of 'innate ideas' given prior to all experience, which reveal the absolute essence of things. Reason is now looked upon rather as an acquisition than as a heritage. It is not the treasury of the mind in which the truth like a minted coin lies stored; it is rather the original intellectual force which guides the discovery and determination of truth. This determination is the seed and the indispensable presupposition of all real certainty. The whole eighteenth century understands reason in this sense; not as a sound body of knowledge, principles, and truths, but as a kind of energy, a force which is fully comprehensible only in its agency and effects. What reason is, and what it can do, can never be known by its results but only by its function. And its most important function consists in its power to bind and to dissolve. It dissolves everything merely factual, all simple data of experience, and everything believed on the evidence of revelation, tradition and authority; and it does not rest content until it has analysed all these things into their simplest component parts and into their last elements of belief and opinion. Following this work of dissolution begins the work of construction. Reason cannot stop with the dispersed parts; it has to build from them a new structure, a true whole. But since reason creates this whole and fits the parts together according to its own rule, it gains complete knowledge of the structure of its product. Reason understands this structure because it can reproduce it in its totality and in the ordered sequence of its individual elements. Only in this twofold intellectual movement can the concept of reason be fully characterized, namely, as a concept of agency, not of being.

The Philosophy of the Enlightenment (Beacon Press, 1951), pp. 6–9, 12–14.

8 The Two Images of Newton

G. BUCHDAHL

What then was the 'Newton-Locke image'? As regards Newton, there are at least two important aspects, codified, as has been suggested, in his two most important works, the *Principia* of 1687 (or, to give its full title in English, *Mathematical Principles of Natural Philosophy*), and the *Opticks* of 1704, 'a treatise of the reflections, refractions ... and colours of light'. The former was a vast synthesis in which all the then-known celestial and terrestrial motions were shown to be derivable from three primary laws of motion together with the law of gravitation, according to which there was a mutual attraction between any two bodies in the universe, of a magnitude that could be expressed by a precise mathematical formula. It was the vastness of this conception, at the same time simple and all-embracing, that caught the imagination of Newton's and later generations.

Let us look at some of the leading features of this work. In the first place, the *content* of Newton's theory involved a synthesis of physical phenomena hitherto believed to be different in *kind*, i.e., those belonging to the sphere of astronomy, and those belonging to that of terrestrial motions. However, not only the content but the very *form* of the *Principia* drove home to the reader an impressive lesson. For this resembled a geometrical treatise such as Euclid's, with its definitions, axioms and theorems, and its very language employed the concepts of geometry proper—straight lines, tangents, ellipses and circles. But unlike Euclid's treatise, the axioms of Newton's book were not self-evident principles about relationships between abstract mathematical quantities. Rather, they were statements, concerning empirical relationships holding between the motions and forces that govern physical phenomena, which (so at least Newton claimed) had been obtained by observation of the phenomena. This synthesis of empirical data and abstract mathematical relations, which here united to lead to accurately verifiable observations, impressed Newton's contemporaries by seemingly bestowing the certainty of mathematics upon man's knowledge of physical phenomena, and gave them a new sense of power over nature.

Two things, then, stand out when we contemplate the form of the *Principia*: the appearance of system, and the mathematisation of natural knowledge. Indeed, the work seemed to suggest that the whole physical universe in some sense mirrored the logical structure of a mathematical theory. Here was the ancestry of the great classical eighteenth-century writings on mechanics, of the works of d'Alembert, Lagrange and Laplace, who brought all the refinements of mathematical analysis to Newton's original ideas, giving the Newtonian system an ever more elegant form which involved less appeal to the visual intuition of the geometer and instead employed a more analytical approach . . . .

If Newton's *Principia* had set the tone in one direction, his *Opticks* was to determine another, exhibiting tendencies in some ways opposed to the first. The *Principia* had been mathematical, involving intricate geometrical relationships together with a highly systematic approach. The *Opticks* was far more discursive and experimental, with detailed accounts of the phenomena of reflexion and refraction, the formation of images by lenses, the mode of operation of the eye, the spectral decomposition of white light, the invention of the reflecting telescope, and so on. Written in English, using little mathematics and less formalism, ending moreover in a series of brilliant speculations (the famous *Queries*, in which the author daringly ranged over many of the subjects that were beginning to interest even the gifted amateur), the book became a focal point of much eighteenth-century writing, both scientific and general.

Whilst the forbidding mathematics of the mechanics of the heavens were gradually driving away the scientific amateur for good and all, the experimental approach of the *Opticks* left at least *some* room for elementary observations, just as it was a formidable stimulus for the imaginative conceptions of the poets of the period. What has been called 'experimental Newtonianism' became an important 'image' for the eighteenth-century thinker and writer. It emphasized observation and experiment, it officially denounced the employment of hypothesis, it stressed the aim of investigating nature at close range, and it ended up by operating *against* the very spirit of systematization which we have seen to be such a central feature of that aspect of eighteenth-century thought so far considered, harking back perhaps more to Greek times and to the seventeenth century rather than pointing towards the future. Whilst the *Principia* was the methodological focus for the systematic thinking of the century in general and the allied sciences of astronomy and dynamics in particular, the *Opticks* in its turn was the stimulus for more down-to-earth experimental researches in the infant sciences of electricity and magnetism and for chemical investigations, even reaching out to biological and geological realms. But if these types of eighteenth-century enquiries thus stress the importance of attending carefully to the experimental aspect, professing a veritable aversion from any sort of speculative ideas, they are none the less very optimistic in their less avowed general presuppositions concerning the innermost fabric of nature, which they usually conceived on atomistic lines. For them, the *Opticks* crystallizes these contradictory strands, exhibiting their conflicting tendencies and holding up opposite faces to its age. The body of the work is concerned with the experimental, and it studiously avoids 'hypotheses', that is, any sort of attempt at explanation; they are 'not to be regarded in experimental philosophy', Newton here tells us. The very first sentence in the body of the *Opticks* sets the stage: 'My Design in this Book is not to explain the Properties of Light by Hypotheses, but to propose and prove them by Reason and Experiments: In order to which I shall premise the following Definitions and Axioms.' We can see that the traditional style is still followed. But the meanings have changed: these 'axioms' are not self-evident truths, not even very fundamental premisses, as had been the laws of motion of the *Principia*, but rather straightforward experimental propositions, 'Principles, for what hath been generally agreed on', as Newton puts it. Coming to the 'theorems', we again find that their 'proofs' usually are 'Proofs by Experiment', and not logical deductions from first principles. But when we turn to the *Queries*, the method changes. There Newton poses a number of questions in which he allows his more speculative frame of mind full sway—brushing aside the constraint put upon the employment of hypotheses. Coming from his hand, these *Queries* were to wield considerable influence. They put his blessing upon the doctrine of the atomic constitution of the universe; they raised important questions in the fields of electrical and chemical studies; and they codified the experimental approach of analysis and synthesis. By this Newton meant that scientific investigations ought to be carried out in a definite order, beginning with experiments and observations; these (when generalized) were to be treated as the effects of certain universal causes

—as, for instance, when he inferred from the motions of the planets the existence of gravitational forces. Then, and only then, was one permitted to reverse this order, using the causes as principles from which one derived and thus explained particular phenomena.

It will be seen that this method allows little scope for the imaginative sweep of the innovator's bold hypotheses; it puts more emphasis on the patient collection of facts, and trusts in the experimenter's ability somehow to see where it will lead him.

The Image of Newton and Locke in the Age of Reason (Sheed and Ward, 1961), pp. 4–15.

IV

Epistemology and Psychology

Like Enlightenment thinkers themselves, Berlin takes the central concern of the age to be the problem of mind. What is the nature of our ideas? And in what sense can we know them to be true? The whole scientific endeavour seemed to depend on some reassuring answers to these questions. But it was the scientific outlook itself which could provide the means of answering. For, if these questions could be translated into empirical terms, if the problem of the nature of knowledge could be transformed into a problem of the origins of ideas, then the same methods which had been so manifestly successful in elucidating the natural world could equally serve to explain the world of the mind. Berlin traces the way in which sensationalist epistemology attempted to give empirical, scientific answers to old philosophic problems. In doing so, he accepts, indeed stresses, the use made by French and English thinkers of the Newtonian example.

9 Science and the Mind

I. BERLIN

If the model that dominated the seventeenth century was mathematical, it is the mechanical model, more particularly that of the Newtonian system, that is everywhere imitated in the century that followed. Philosophical questions are in fact *sui generis*, and resemble questions of mechanics no more closely than those of mathematics (or of biology or psychology or history); nevertheless the effect upon philosophy of one model is very different from that of another . . . .

The eighteenth century is perhaps the last period in the history of

Western Europe when human omniscience was thought to be an attainable goal. The unparalleled progress of physics and mathematics in the previous century transformed the generally held view of the nature of the material world, and, still more, of the nature of true knowledge, to such a degree, that this epoch still stands like a barrier between us and the ages which preceded it, and makes the philosophical ideas of the Middle Ages, and even the Renaissance, seem remote, fanciful and, at times, almost unintelligible. The application of mathematical techniques—and language—to the measurable properties of what the senses revealed, became the sole true method of discovery and of exposition. Descartes and Spinoza, Leibniz and Hobbes, all seek to give their reasoning a structure of a mathematical kind. What can be said must be statable in quasi-mathematical terms, for language less precise may turn out to conceal the fallacies and obscurities, the confused mass of superstitions and prejudices, which characterized the discredited theological or other forms of dogmatic doctrine about the universe, which the new science had come to sweep away and supersede. This mood persists into the eighteenth century, with Newton's influence as the strongest single factor. Newton had performed the unprecedented task of explaining the material world, that is, of making it possible, by means of relatively few fundamental laws of immense scope and power, to determine, at least in principle, the properties and behaviour of every particle of every material body in the universe, and that with a degree of precision and simplicity undreamt of before. Order and clarity now reigned in the realm of physical science:

> Nature and Nature's Laws lay hid in Night:
> God said, Let Newton be! and all was Light!

Yet the ancient disciplines of metaphysics, logic, ethics, and all that related to the social life of men, still lay in chaos, governed by the confusions of thought and language of an earlier and unregenerate age. It was natural, and indeed almost inevitable, that those who had been liberated by the new sciences should seek to apply their methods and principles to a subject which was clearly in even more desperate need of order than the facts of the external world. Indeed this task was of crucial importance: for without a true and clear picture of the principal 'faculties' and operations of the human mind, one could not be certain how much credence to give to various types of thought or reasoning, nor how to determine the sources and limits of human knowledge, nor the relationships between its varieties. But unless this was known the claims of ignoramuses and charlatans could not be properly exposed; nor the new picture of the material world adequately related to other matters of interest to men—moral conduct, aesthetic principles, laws of history and of social and political life, the 'inner' workings of the passions and the imagination, and all the other issues of central interest to human beings. A science of nature had been created; a science of mind had yet to be made. The goal in both cases must remain the same: the formulation of general laws on the basis of observation ('inner' and 'outer'), and, when necessary, experiment; and the deduction from such laws, when established, of specific conclusions. To every genuine question there were many false answers, and only one true one; once discovered it was final—it remained for ever true; all that was needed was a reliable method of discovery. A method which answered to this description had been employed by 'the incomparable Mr Newton'; his emulators in the realm of the human mind would reap a harvest no less rich if they followed similar precepts. If the laws were correct, the observations upon which they were based authentic, and the inferences sound, true and impregnable conclusions would provide knowledge of hitherto unexplored realms, and transform the present welter of ignorance and idle conjecture into a clear and coherent system of logically interrelated elements—the theoretical copy or analogue of the divine harmony of nature, concealed from the view by human ignorance or idleness or perversity. To comprehend it, is, for a rational creature, tantamount to conforming to it in all one's beliefs and actions; for this alone can make men happy and rational and free.

It was essential to guarantee the efficacy of the instruments of investigation before its results could be trusted. This epistemological bias characterized European philosophy from Descartes' formulation of his method of doubt until well into the nineteenth century, and is still a strong tendency in it. The direct application of the results of this investigation of the varieties and scope of human knowledge to such traditional disciplines as politics, ethics, metaphysics, theology, and so on, with a view to ending their perplexities once and for all, is the programme which philosophers of the eighteenth century attempted to carry through. The principles which they attempted to apply were the new scientific canons of the seventeenth century; there was to be no *a priori* deduction from 'natural' principles, hallowed in the Middle Ages, without experimental evidence, such as that all bodies come to rest when no longer under the influence of any force, or that the 'natural' path sought after by heavenly bodies, in the quest for self-fulfilment, is necessarily circular. The laws of Kepler or Galileo contradicted these 'natural' principles, on the basis of observation (the vast mass of data, for instance, accumulated by the Danish astronomer Tycho Brahe), and experiment (of the kind conducted by Galileo himself). This use of observation and experiment entailed the application of exact methods of measurement, and resulted in the linking together of many diverse phenomena under laws of great precision, generally formulated in mathematical terms. Consequently only the measurable aspects of reality were to be treated as real—those susceptible to equations connecting the variations in one aspect of a phenomenon with measurable variations in other phenomena. The whole notion of nature as compounded of irreducibly different qualities and unbridgeable 'natural' kinds, was to be finally discarded. The Aristotelian category of final cause—the explanation of phenomena in terms of the 'natural' tendency of every object to fulfil its own inner end or purpose—which was also to be the answer to the question of why it existed, and what function it was attempting to fulfil—notions for which no experimental or observational evidence can in principle be discovered—was abandoned as unscientific, and, indeed, in the case of inanimate entities without wills or purposes, as literally unintelligible. Laws formulating regular concomitances of phenomena—the observed order and conjunctions of things and events—were sufficient, without introducing impalpable entities and forces, to describe all that is describable, and predict all that is predictable, in the universe. Space, time, mass, force, momentum, rest—the terms of mechanics—are to take the place of final causes, substantial forms, divine purpose, and other metaphysical notions. Indeed the apparatus of medieval ontology and theology were to be altogether abandoned in favour of a symbolism referring to those aspects of the universe which are given to the senses, or can be measured or inferred in some other way.

This attitude is exceedingly clear in the works not only of Locke and Hume, who had a profound respect for natural science, but also in those of Berkeley, who was deeply concerned to deny its metaphysical presuppositions. To all of them the model was that of contemporary physics and mechanics. The world of matter for Newton, and indeed for those pre-Newtonian physicists with whose works Locke was probably acquainted rather better, was to be described in terms of uniform particles, and the laws of its behaviour were the laws of the interaction of these particles. The British empiricist philosophers, whose work gradually came to dominate European thought, applied this conception to the mind. The mind was treated as if it were a box containing mental equivalents of the Newtonian particles. These were called 'ideas'. These 'ideas' are distinct and separate entities, 'simple', i.e., possessing no parts into which they can be split, that is, literally atomic, having their origin somewhere in the external world, dropping into the mind like so many grains of sand inside an hour glass; there, in some way, they either continue in isolation, or are compounded to form complexes, in the way in which material objects in the outer world are compounded out of complexes of molecules or atoms. Locke attempts something like the history of the genesis of ideas in our minds and an account of their movement within it, their association and dissociation from each other, like a contemporary chemist analysing the ingredients and physical behaviour of a compound substance. Thought, at least reflective thought, is for Locke a kind of inner eye, corresponding to the outer physical eye which takes in the external world. When Locke defines knowledge as 'the perception of the connection and agreement or disagreement and repugnancy of any of our ideas', this 'perception' is conceived by him as something which inspects two ideas as if they were discriminable particles; the inner eye is then able to see whether they agree or not, and so whether the proposition asserting their connection is or is not true, much as the outer eye can inspect two coloured objects and see whether the colours match each other or not. When Berkeley criticizes Locke's theory of abstract general ideas, what he is principally attacking is the notion that there can be an idea which is not an absolutely determinate image, since ideas are entities; and 'abstract ideas', as invoked by Locke in order to explain how general terms mean, seem to Berkeley a contradiction in terms, because if they are ideas, they must be concrete entities, and cannot also be abstract, that is, not determinate, not having any particular properties given to the senses or the imagination. Whether his attack upon Locke is fair or not, what is characteristic is the assumption common to both (and to Hume and many other contemporary empiricists, particularly in France) that the mind is a container within which ideas like counters circulate and form patterns as they would in a complicated slot machine; three-dimensional Newtonian space has its counterpart in the inner 'space' of the mind over which the inner eye—the faculty of reflection—presides.

Philosophy, therefore, is to be converted into a natural science. The facts with which it is to deal are to be discovered by introspection. Like every other genuine human investigation it must begin with empirical observation. Hume echoes this: 'As the science of man is the only solid foundation for the other science, so the only solid foundation we can give to this science itself must be laid on experience and observation.' Philosophy is in reality a kind of scientific psychology; among the extreme followers of this doctrine, particularly in France, it becomes a kind of physiology—an early version of behaviourism or 'physicalism'. The French disciples of Locke and Hume, Condillac, Helvétius, La Mettrie, push this to extreme limits. Condillac undertakes to reconstruct every human experience—the most complex and sophisticated thoughts or 'movements of the soul', the most elaborate play of the imagination, the most subtle scientific speculation—out of 'simple' ideas, that is, sensations classifiable as being given to one or the other of our normal senses, each of which can, as it were, be pin-pointed and assigned to its rightful place in the stream of sensations. The great popularizers of the age, whose writings reached educated readers in many lands beyond the borders of their native France, headed by Voltaire, Diderot, Holbach, Condorcet, and their followers, whatever their other differences, were agreed upon the crucial importance of this sensationalist approach. There are 'organic'—anti-atomic—notions in the writings of Diderot as well as those of Maupertuis or Bordeu, and some of these may have influenced Kant; but the dominant trend is in favour of analysing everything into ultimate, irreducible atomic constituents, whether physical or psychological. Hume, who believes 'that the sciences of mathematics and natural philosophy (i.e., natural science) and natural religion have such a dependence on the knowledge of man', believes this because the task of philosophy is to deal with the ultimate ingredients of all that there is. His theory of the mind is mechanistic, and conceived by analogy with Newton's theory of gravitational attraction, the association of ideas being called upon to perform the same function in the mind as gravitation does in the material world. This association of ideas is described by him as 'a kind of attraction, which in the mental world will be found to have as extraordinary effects as in the natural, and to show itself in as many and as various forms'. La Mettrie conceives the true philosopher as a kind of engineer who can take to pieces the apparatus that is the human mind; Voltaire describes him as an excellent anatomist, who (he is speaking in praise of Locke) can explain human reason as he can explain the springs of the human body. Scientific images abound in the philosophical treatises of the French *philosophes* and their disciples in other countries; Nature, which was conceived as an organism by Butler in the beginning of the century, was compared to a watch by Dean Paley half a century later. 'Natural morality' and 'natural religion' (common to all men, but more evident in the least corrupt—rural or primitive—societies) can be studied scientifically like the life of plants or animals. Diderot compares social life to a great workshop factory.[1]

The Age of Enlightenment (Mentor, 1956), pp. 14–20.

V
Religion

Maistre's caricature of the *philosophes* as irreligious conspirators, intent on subverting both divine and human authority, ignores the variety of their religious positions. Nevertheless, it does point to some truths. Whilst the bulk of the population remained firmly of the faith, there was, at any rate in France, a gradual separation of intellectual authority and orthodox Christianity. Yet there was no intellectual coherence amongst the protestants, no orthodoxy of unorthodoxy. In particular, there was a split between deists, with Voltaire at their head, and atheists such as La Mettrie and d'Holbach relying on materialist doctrines. Hazard, in his *European Thought in the Eighteenth Century*, disentangles this fraternal controversy. Deism never had the intellectual force in England that it had in France. Leslie Stephen suggests that, whilst in France a dogmatic and persecuting Church created in reaction an equally rigid scepticism, in England a tolerant Church, already itself affected by rationalism, could offer shelter to most shades of opinion which fell short of outright deism.

10 Natural Religion

P. HAZARD

The City of Men should be built on simple lines. The first thing to be done was to clear the site of the miscellaneous jumble of buildings that encumbered it. Even the old foundations would have to go, for nothing really satisfactory had ever been erected on them. Once the ground was cleared and levelled, honest, sensible buildings would be put up. The new builders would in no way be bound by the past, nor would they waste their time trying to put right this or that detail of the old structures. That would take too long. Their work would be to plan a kind of building thoroughly suited to the needs of people who would now cease to live in Babel, and cease to hope for the attainment of some problematical heaven.

A single word sufficed to put heart into the daring ones who were making ready to begin the task; yet another talisman, in addition to those with which we are already familiar, Reason and Knowledge. That new, that magic word was Nature. To it they ascribed a virtue more potent than any, since Nature was the source of Knowledge and the touchstone of Reason. Nature was wise, and Nature was kindly. Let man but render a willing ear to Nature, and never more would he go astray. All he had to do was to obey her kindly mandate.

So, as a first step, Religion should be based on Nature; not only because religion, properly understood, was but an emanation of Nature, but also because it would be one with that instinct which Nature implants in us, enabling us by its means to distinguish truth from falsehood and good from evil; and yet again because, instead of teaching us to look on our earthly life as a time of trial, it would conform to Nature, whose aim it is not to make trial of us, but to make us happy. Long since, its coming had been foretold by the prophets, and slowly but surely, out of sight, far underground, and unsuspected by the mass of mankind, it had been making ready. And now, behold, it was coming forth into the light of day. It was not so much the substance of it, as its arrogance, its audacity, and its eagerness to proselytize that made it seem so startling a prodigy.

God was to remain, but a God so remote, so watered down, so pallid that his presence imposed no constraint on the City of Men. He would neither visit them with his wrath, nor bedazzle them with his glory. Deism and theism required no act of faith. The process involved was a purely intellectual one, culminating in one simple and satisfying conclusion, namely that God exists. We have but to glance at Creation as a whole to recognize how admirably it works. But we cannot imagine effects without a cause; therefore we must take it that a primary cause exists. A clock implies the existence of a clockmaker. Well, we have before us what we may compare to a well-regulated clock; therefore there must be somewhere the skilful craftsman who made it and who keeps it in order. That craftsman is God.

What was it that led God to create the world out of nothing? The question is an embarrassing one. But it would be still more embarrassing to have to suppose that the world came into existence by chance, that it works by chance, and that it exists for no special purpose. It would be tantamount to saying that reasoning beings were created without the intervention of reason. Let us be sensible, and prefer the difficult to the absurd. Let us accept the theory of final causes. A makeshift conclusion, which still does duty.

Deism had recourse to a sort of filtering process. If we strain off whatever strikes us as superstitious in the Church of Rome, in the reformed Church, and in every other church and sect, what remains at the conclusion of the process will be God; a God whom we know not, and whom we cannot know. Hardly anything has been left to him save the bare fact of his existence. Of all the possible adjectives, he was awarded the one which was at once the most honourable and the most vague; he was called the Supreme Being.

What is the good of sacraments, of religious rites, of churches, temples and mosques? The Isle of Reason shall have a beauty all its own, a beauty that can dispense with domes and towers. What good are priests and pastors? There is but one way to worship God, and that is to worship him inwardly, with heart and mind and soul. To acknowledge in a general sort of way a primary and Supreme Being; to lift up our hearts to him from time to time; to abstain from whatever is deemed dishonourable in the land in which we dwell, to fulfil certain prescribed social duties—these are the essential things; anything else is merely supererogatory. There is no need for pious observances. Such things do but distract the mind from the true object of worship. Taken up with listening to sermons, people forget all about helping their neighbour . . . .

They hoped that the idea of an ever-living God which they thus preserved would win them a Catholicity vaster than any which Catholicism itself had ever attained. They argued that, because the Christian religion had started at a comparatively recent date, and because it had only been promulgated among a minority of the peoples of the earth, it laboured under a twofold limitation. Deism, on the other hand, drew its adherents from the whole expanse of Time and Space. We claim (they gave out) that our religion is as old as the world. . . .

What sort of a part did the atheists play, side by side with the deists? . . .

The general background against which these extremists stood out gradually became less strongly contrasted with their negations. The atheist was no longer held to be an unmitigated criminal. He was graciously allowed some extenuating qualities. It was thought that he might quite possibly be the victim of a delusion, and that he erred in good faith. In point of fact, people told themselves, there were two

kinds of atheists, two distinct brands. There were the vicious and immoral sort, who were against religion because it condemned their mode
of life. These, of course, were the bad ones. But were there not other
atheists, quite distinct from these, of quite another kidney? Were there
not some worthy and respectable atheists, who loved whatsoever was
good, commendable and fair? They loved their fellow men, they were
good members of society, and, if they had acquired some regrettable
notions, it was really their native good sense that was at the root of it all;
that was the real explanation. They had been suckled on superstition at
their nurse's breast, and ever since then they had mistaken religion for
superstition. It was to be deplored, but it was understandable. After all,
it was easier to get an atheist on to the right road than an enthusiast, or
a fanatic. . . .

There was a tendency, a drift, towards philosophic materialism.
Mind was wholly distinct from matter. That was an established fact.
Yet two men attacked it. One of them was Locke, who was anxious to
remain a Christian; the other was Voltaire, who adhered firmly to his
deism. There have been cases of ideas being twisted, and even completely misinterpreted, and then, from that very distortion, deriving
their subsequent success. Here is an idea that eluded its inventor and put
him in an unwelcome position: though designed to illustrate the omnipotence of God, its real effect was to confound mind and matter, and to
prove to the satisfaction of a whole school of philosophers, the un-
soundness of what they termed the soul-hypothesis . . . .

And now for a move towards scientific materialism. All life, say the
scientists, manifests itself through matter and through matter alone.
Thus do the scientists come to the support of these enterprising philosophers, on whom, however, they look a little superciliously. They
regarded them a little scornfully, as being people who were satisfied
with mere verbiage. They pretended, these philosophers, to deal with
facts and nothing but facts, yet when it came to the point, they made
the whole business a mere matter of word-spinning. These learned
scientists, on the other hand, spoke as observers who kept their eyes on
Nature, on the living thing, and knew precisely what it was. If they
kept on turning out book after book on the question whether or not
animals had souls, it was because they thought that the supporters of
the spiritual theory supplied them with a valuable argument: organic
creatures can exist without souls, and yet live quite satisfactorily. Epicurus and his system, with its atoms and its combination of atoms;
those innumerable throws of the dice which at last combined in such

a manner as to produce the world—all this was still dear to their minds. Nevertheless, these various theories did not seem altogether able to account for the phenomenon of life. They required to be overhauled, brought up to date. And that was what several somewhat eccentric gentlemen decided to do. . . .

Most clamorous of them all [was] La Mettrie. Materialism, he shouted with all the force of his lungs, materialism is the way to salvation, materialism is the truth. We must start with Nature, a power devoid of knowledge and of feeling, as blind when she bestows life as when she takes it away. How does she go about her work? Does she create seeds of every species which are scattered throughout the universe till at last they meet together? Or does she proceed by way of an evolutionary process, the early generations imperfect or monstrous, those alone surviving in whom no essential organ is lacking? What is undeniable is that all our anatomical and physiological experiments go to show that, what we are pleased to call the soul is nothing but an appanage of the body. Its manifestations are, in fact, determined by the different states of the body; it is affected by illness, it is soothed by opium, it is excited by coffee or wine, hunger makes it cruel and savage, it has its successive periods of growth, maturity and decay; it changes as it grows old, and it varies according to climate. In short, it has no existence apart from matter; it *is* matter. It is a vague term, without any definite meaning behind it; a word by which we denote the thinking part of us. Thought is merely a property of organic matter, like electricity, or the faculty of motion, or impenetrability, or extent. Its study is a branch of natural history, *Histoire naturelle* of the soul (1745). There is nothing in man to differentiate him from the purely mechanical character of all other living things; *L'homme machine* (1747). Being a machine made to feel, to think, to know good from bad, as you know blue from yellow; in a word, to be born with an understanding, and a sure moral instinct, all this has nothing more out-of-the-way about it than being a monkey, or a parrot, or in knowing the things you like. Or, if you prefer it, man is a plant, for plants, too, are machines: *L'homme plante* (1748): 'Anyone who looked on man as a plant was no more uncomplimentary to that noble species than he who regarded him as a mere machine. Man grows in the womb by a process of vegetation; his body runs down and is wound up again like a watch, either by its own recuperative power, which often works satisfactorily, or by the skill of people who understand it, not in this instance watch-and-clock-makers, but biochemists.' And we must needs be fatalists: 'We are no more committing a crime when we obey our primitive instincts, than the Nile is committing a crime with its floods, or the sea with its ravages.' Nay, we ought rather to be pleased: 'Do you know why I still retain some respect for mankind? It is because I seriously look on them as machines. If I did not, I know but few whom I should regard as very desirable companions. Materialism is the cure for misanthropy.' . . .

Against the atheists, the deists piled argument upon argument, contesting their conclusions, one after another. Experiment shows, said the atheists, that when portions of matter which we had supposed to be inert and inanimate are combined in a certain way, they become active and endowed with life and intelligence: that is false, say the deists. Matter and motion suffice to explain everything. Not so. Matter is eternal and necessary. It is not. When you say you are going to prove that there is no God, that matter acts of itself, by eternal necessity, you are bound to prove it as clearly as you would a proposition in Euclid, otherwise all your theories are but founded on a peradventure. What a foundation for a thing which concerns mankind more deeply than any other imaginable.

But the atheists did not give in. They had the same scorn for deism as the deists had for Christianity. 'A materialist once said to me that a deist was the sort of man who was not weak enough to be a Christian and not strong enough to be an atheist.' Some excitable female philosopher is said to have declared that Voltaire, being a deist, was necessarily a bigot. What did they mean, these feeble creatures, these 'final cause' apostles, by a religion without mystery? Surely, that was a contradiction in terms. And how prevaricating to go on worshipping a God, of whom, on their own confession, they were unable to form the slightest conception. The difference between the God of the deist, the optimist, the enthusiast and the God of the devout, the credulous and the zealot was entirely a matter of feeling and temperament. From deism to superstition is never more than a step. Of the deist, as of everyone else who professes a religion, we might appropriately say, *Ecce homo;* whereas the real man, the man who never bends the knee to anyone, in other words the atheist, we should greet with an *Ecce vir.*

Thus did these *quondam* allies, who once thought to make common cause against a common foe, call each other over the coals, and in no honeyed terms. It now began to be borne in upon them more and more clearly, that their ideas were fundamentally divergent.

Taking it on the whole, the eighteenth century was deistic rather than atheistic; but, however unwillingly, it was compelled to make room for an atheism which taxed it with the same sort of timidity as that with which the deists had taxed the Christians.

European Thought in the Eighteenth Century (Hollis and Carter, 1954), pp. 113–29.

11 Deism in England and France

L. STEPHEN

Here, then, is the starting-point of the deist controversy. From the variation of opinions Bossuet inferred that all, save one, should be stamped out. The inevitable tendency of such a method was already seen by the more acute minds. To support a religion by force instead of argument is to admit that argument condemns it. In other words, it is to sanction scepticism; and before the end of the coming century, Bossuet's countrymen had to reap the harvest of which the seeds were sown by this desperate policy. The English theologians, accustomed to trust in reason, though with some heterogeneous admixture of tradition, and to practise toleration, though with many limitations, adopted a different course. Since men differ hopelessly on many points, let us take that in which all agree. That surely must be the essence of religion and the teaching of universal reason. Thus we shall be able to found a reasonable Christianity. You must go further, said the deists, and take only the axioms common to all men. Thus we shall found, if not a reasonable Christianity, yet a religion of reason. The various eddies of opinion which were formed by the conflict of these diverging currents form the staple of the theological discussions of the coming period.

One result of the English toleration and rationalism, and it may be, of the English love of compromise, necessarily affected the process of thought. In England, in fact, theology had become so profoundly penetrated with rationalism, that the attempt to frame a permanent reconciliation had a far more hopeful appearance than in Catholic countries. The result was that the most eminent English thinkers were generally arrayed upon the orthodox side. They could find liberty enough to satisfy their logical instincts within the old lines; and saw no sufficient advantage in pushing forwards into the unknown regions of Deism. The orthodox party had thus every advantage which could be given by ability, learning, and prestige. It would be difficult to mention a controversy in which there was a greater disparity of force. The physiognomy of the books themselves bears marks of the difference. The deist writings are but shabby and shrivelled little octavos, generally anonymous, such as lurk in the corners of dusty shelves, and seem to be the predestined prey of moths. Against them are arrayed solid octavos and handsome quartos and at times even folios—very Goliaths among books, too ponderous for the indolence of our degenerate days, but fitting representatives of the learned dignitaries who compiled them. On the side of Christianity, indeed, appeared all that was intellectually venerable in England. . . .

[The deists] are but a ragged regiment, whose whole ammunition of learning was a trifle when compared with the abundant stores of a single light of orthodoxy; whilst in speculative ability most of them were children by the side of their ablest antagonists. Swift's sneering assertion, that their literary power would hardly have attracted attention if employed upon any other topic, seems to be generally justified. . . .

The deists suffered from another disadvantage besides their intellectual infirmity. They had to fight in fetters. Toleration, acknowledged in theory, was not yet pushed to its legitimate consequences. The English mind had arrived at one of its favourite compromises. The Church of England could no longer persecute, but it was still privileged. A dissenter was disqualified for office, though not regarded as a criminal. Near a century and a half was to elapse from the revolution which had given him a legal right to freedom of worship before the rights of other citizens were avowedly conferred upon him. The infidel was a degree lower. He was still liable to persecution, though seldom persecuted in practice. Even Locke had drawn the line of toleration above atheists and Roman Catholics, and certain laws—some of them not even yet repealed—made open assailants or orthodox Christianity liable to severe penalties. Occasionally the weapon, generally held in suspense above the heads of free-thinkers, was allowed to descend, though with little severity, and pretty much at random. It was perfectly safe, and in some classes fashionable, to express sceptical opinions in conversation, but it was clearly disreputable, and not quite safe to publish them. If the governing classes hated priestcraft, and cared little for Christianity, they had a great value for decorum. A wretched man, called Aikenhead was executed in Scotland, in the beginning of 1697, for some profane language to the students in Edinburgh, though he afterwards recanted and averred his belief in Christianity. But in England little harm was done. The deist books were occasionally burnt by the hangman, which probably served as an advertisement. Collins at one time thought it necessary to retire to Holland; poor Asgill was expelled from Parliament and ruined, for denying the necessity of death. Whiston lost his professorship for Arianism; Woolston was fined and imprisoned for language more significant of insanity than of intentional profanity; and at a later period Annet was pilloried and imprisoned for equally insulting language. But, as a rule, the deists escaped without injury; their creed exposed them to much obloquy, but little danger; and they were forced, not to conceal their opinions, but to cover them with a veil of decent ambiguity. Some of them have, in consequence, been regarded as sincere believers, and, on the other hand, they have been condemned for insidious dishonesty. The question of how far they saw the consequences of their own logic is of little interest to the historian of thought. We shall have to notice it incidentally hereafter.

When the sceptical movement had passed from England to France the disparity of intellect was inverted. Voltaire, the disciple of the English deists, found no disciple of Butler or Bentley to encounter him with equal ability. The persecution, on the other hand, by which the French movement was opposed was of a far more serious character. The two phenomena are naturally connected. In England, the rational Protestant could meet the deist half-way. The line of demarcation was shifting and uncertain, and it is hard to say in many cases whether the old traditional element, or the modern rationalizing element, predominates. Persecution would be anomalous between sects so faintly discriminated. In Catholic France a rigid and unbending system was confronted by a thoroughgoing scepticism. Men of intellect could find no half-way resting-place, and could disguise their true sentiments with no shreds of orthodox belief. What passed for Christianity in England would have been rank heresy in France; and thus the Catholic Church, unable to come to terms with the rationalists, met them by a free use of the weapons of authority. It is generally added that in England the orthodox party, forced to defend themselves by reason, won a triumph in argument as conclusive as might be expected from their superiority in learning and ability. Whatever the truth of that boast, it is certain that the deist impulse showed rapid signs of decay. Burke could ask before the end of the century, 'Who ever reads them now?' and even at a much earlier period the decline is palpable. 'What is become of all those poisonous books,' asks Seed before 1750, 'that were written about the close of the last century, nay of some of much later date?'

English Thought in the Eighteenth Century (Hart-Davis, 1962) pp. 71–5.

VI

Optimism and the Problem of Evil

That the *philosophes* were naïve, gullible and simplistic rationalists, blind disciples of the faith of reason, arrogant and presumptuous believers in the powers of men to reconstitute men, this has been an axiom common to many interpretations of the Enlightenment from Burke on. This view ignores the caution and moderation of some of the central figures of the age, such as Montesquieu; it leaves aside the degree to which the appeal to reason coincided with a conviction of its limitations; it overlooks the weakening of rationalist thought in both its natural law and utilitarian forms by the development of subjectivism and anti-rationalism. As Lovejoy showed in his seminal work *The Great Chain of Being*, it disregards also the essential pessimism and quietism of philosophic optimism. Above all, it glosses over the tensions, doubts and ambiguities involved in the loss of Christian faith and the secularization of thought. This darker side, this hesitation and perplexity, has been taken into account by Crocker and Gay. As the title of one of his books, *The Age of Crisis*, suggests, Crocker regards the eighteenth century as a crucial period when most of the typical intellectual features of the modern world were imprinted on the European mind. The challenge to Christian authority raised many problems, the foremost of which was to build new yet stable foundations for old values. Despite the vigour of the attempts to restore and reinvigorate moral and intellectual certainties, the logic of the challenge led to the denial of all values. By way of this argument, Crocker can pick on the Marquis de Sade as a central figure of the age and trace to it the nihilism which he believes lies behind the political breakdown of the twentieth century. For Gay too the secularization of thought and the genuine anguish it created are crucial aspects of Enlightenment thought. Yet, perhaps because he has not so easily abandoned rationalist hopes, his interpretation is more sociological and less apocalyptic than Crocker's. The doubts and torments besetting the *philosophes* did not arise from difficulties in the very structure of their thought; they were the tensions felt by men at ease in their world who nevertheless were led by their ideas to trouble both themselves and their society.

12 Eighteenth-Century Optimism

A. O. LOVEJOY

The common thesis of eighteenth-century optimists was, as is notorious, the proposition that this is the best of possible worlds; and this fact, together with the connotation which the term 'optimism' has come to assume in popular usage, has given rise to the belief that the adherents of this doctrine must have been exuberantly cheerful persons, fatuously blind to the realities of human experience and of human nature, or insensible to all the pain and frustration and conflict which are manifest through the entire range of sentient life. Yet there was in fact nothing in the optimist's creed which logically required him either to blink or to belittle the facts which we ordinarily call evil. So far from asserting the unreality of evils, the philosophical optimist in the eighteenth century was chiefly occupied in demonstrating their necessity. To assert that this is the best of possible worlds implies nothing as to the absolute goodness of this world; it implies only that any other world which is metaphysically capable of existence would be worse. The reasoning of the optimist was directed less to showing how much of what men commonly reckon good there is in the world of reality than to showing how little of it there is in the world of possibility—in that eternal logical order which contains the Ideas of all things possible and compossible, which the mind of God was conceived to have contemplated 'before the creation', and by the necessities of which, ineluctable even by Omnipotence, his creative power was restricted.

At bottom, indeed, optimism had much in common with that Manichaean dualism, against Bayle's defence of which so many of the theodicies were directed. Optimism too, as Leibniz acknowledged, had its two antagonistic 'principles'. The role of the 'evil principle' was simply assigned to the divine reason, which imposed singular impediments upon the benevolent intentions of the divine will. The very ills which Bayle had argued must be attributed to the interference of a species of extraneous Anti-God, for whose existence and hostility to the good no rational explanation could be given, were by the optimist attributed to a necessity inhering in the nature of things; and it was questionable whether this was not the less cheerful view of the two. For it was possible to hope that in the fullness of time the Devil might be put under foot, and believers in revealed religion were assured that he would be; but logical necessities are eternal, and the evils which arise from them must therefore be perpetual. Thus eighteenth-century optimism not only had affinities with the dualism to which it was supposed to be antithetic, but the arguments of its advocates at times sounded strangely like those of the pessimist—a type by no means unknown in the period. The moral was different, but the view of the concrete facts of experience was sometimes very much the same; since it was the optimist's contention that evil—and a great deal of it—is involved in the general constitution of things, he found it to his purpose to dilate, on occasion, upon the magnitude of the sum of evil and upon the depth and breadth of its penetration into life. . . .

In short the writings of the optimists afforded abundant ground for Voltaire's exclamation:

> Vous criez 'Tout est bien' d'une voix lamentable!

Voltaire's chief complaint of these philosophers in the *Poem on the Lisbon Disaster* was not, as has often been supposed, that they were too indecently cheerful, that their view of the reality of evil was superficial; his complaint was that they were too depressing, that they made the actual evils we experience appear yet worse by representing them as inevitable and inherent in the permanent structure of the universe.

> Non, ne présentez plus a mon coeur agité
> Ces immuables lois de la nécessité!

An evil unexplained seemed to Voltaire more endurable than the same evil explained, when the explanation consisted in showing that from all eternity the avoidance of just that evil had been, and through all eternity the avoidance of others like it would be, logically inconceivable. In this his own feeling, and his assumption about the psychology of the emotions in other men, were precisely opposite to Spinoza's, who believed that everything becomes endurable to us when we once see clearly that it never could have been otherwise: *quatenus mens res omnes ut necessarias intelligit, eatenus minus ab affectibus patitur.* Though most of the optimistic writers of the eighteenth century were less thoroughgoing or less frank in their cosmical determinism than Spinoza, such philosophic consolation as they offered was at bottom the same as his.

It was an essentially intellectual consolation; the mood that it was usually designed to produce was that of reasoned acquiescence in the inevitable, based upon a conviction that its inevitableness was absolute and due to no arbitrary caprice; or, at a higher pitch, a devout willingness to be damned—that is, to be as much damned as one was—for the better demonstration of the reasonableness of the general scheme of things. Whether confronted with physical or with moral evils, wrote Pope, 'to reason well is to submit'; and again:

> Know thy own point; this kind, this due degree,
> Of blindness, weakness, Heaven bestows on thee.
> Submit!

It is, of course, true that the optimistic writers were eager to show that good comes out of evil; but what it was indispensable for them to establish was that it could come in no other way. It is true, also, that they were wont, when they reached the height of their argument, to discourse with eloquence on the perfection of the Universal System as a whole; but that perfection in no way implied either the happiness or the excellence of the finite parts of the system. On the contrary, the fundamental and characteristic premise of the usual proof of optimism was the proposition that the perfection of the whole depends upon, indeed consists in, the existence of every possible degree of imperfection in the parts. Voltaire, once more, summarized the argument not altogether unjustly when he wrote:

> Vous composerez dans ce chaos fatal
> Des malheurs de chaque être un bonheur général.

The essence of the optimist's enterprise was to find the evidence of the 'goodness' of the universe not in the paucity but rather in the multiplicity of what to the unphilosophic mind appeared to be evils.

The Great Chain of Being (Harper Torchbook, 1960), pp. 208-11

13 The Problem of Evil

L. G. CROCKER

Of the many abstract questions that exercised the curiosity of eighteenth century thinkers—happiness, luxury, progress, man and beast, truth and falsehood, and so on—none evoked more universal and heated debate than the problem of evil, with the possible exception of freedom of the will. As Diderot wrote in his article 'Manichéisme', 'It must be admitted, of all the questions that occur to the mind, it is the most difficult and thorny.' Voltaire, anguished by it, cried, 'Here is the most difficult and important of questions. All of human life is involved.' What was really involved was a direct attack on the existence of God, to begin with, and an assessment of his nature. Beyond these primary issues, the relation between man and God, the doctrines of providence and moral freedom, and ultimately, the Divine sanction for ethical values were inseparable parts of the debate.

The dilemma of God's goodness and omnipotence, set off against a world of ills, evils and injustice, was not new to the Age of Enlightenment. As far back as men have reflected on themselves and the world they live in, they have speculated about their relation to the superior powers they conceived to have created the universe and to direct it. When they reached a point of rational maturity at which they could objectify both themselves and their world in somewhat abstract terms, they began to be tormented by the problem of evil. In two ancient cultures it found lofty expression—with a diversity of answers—in the Book of Job and the Greek tragedies. Christianity had tried to resolve the problem, at least in part, by the doctrine of the Fall, which made evil an obstacle, incurred freely by man, that he had to overcome.

The eighteenth century, precisely because it was an age of enlightenment, had to re-examine and thrash out anew the age-old problem. In a period of independent and rebellious rationalism, no authoritarian answers could be accepted without questioning. As mastery over the physical world seemed more and more a certainty, many no longer felt the need to fall back on faith to explain their misery. In the new scientific and secular outlook, the Fall became a myth, unrelated to known phenomena. The obsession with happiness that characterized the eighteenth century, and the change in the social and moral climate after the death of Louis XIV also helped turn people away from the traditional Christian patience with suffering on this earth. Besides, as we have seen in the first chapter, many important questions could not be solved without taking the problem of evil into account. The eighteenth century, as Pope clearly acknowledged, felt obliged 'to vindicate the ways of God to man'. . .

The materialists . . . denied the metaphysical reality of evil, and the very existence of a 'problem of evil', inasmuch as the universe is simply empty of moral value. This view is basic to La Mettrie, Helvétius, d'Holbach and Diderot. The materialist's answer to the disaster of

Lisbon was superficially like that of the Christian optimist; more profoundly, it was quite different. This *is* the best of all possible worlds, they granted, because it is the only possible world. The materialists did not approve of Robinet's equilibrium, however. Good and bad are variables. Yet all is good as it can be, because all is necessarily determined. Good and evil are realities, but only, as Spinoza had said, in terms of an individual's experience. It is not true that evil, as certain optimists claimed, is a mere appearance, an error in the human mind, or that partial evil gives rise to universal good. But it is true, as many apologists contended, that physical evil is a result of the laws of matter, and that moral evil stems from self-love—which, however, is necessary to preservation, and so a good. Hunger, said Diderot, is necessary, and so are passions (which result from sensitivity). While for the Christian optimist this evil was necessary in the best of possible worlds, for Diderot it was necessary because this is the only possible world. 'All is good' is false; but we may say, 'All that is, is necessary,' or 'All is the best it can be'. . . .

For the eighteenth century materialist, then, the universe is not moral, and our purely human evaluations have no meaning in reference to it, no status in being. Voltaire was wrong to apply moral categories in his consideration. Certainly, if there is a 'problem of evil', then it is impossible to avoid metaphysics and theology; and so Voltaire who hated metaphysics, became embroiled in it, as did Rousseau. Diderot's contribution lay in pointing out that there is no such problem. There can be none, unless we postulate, first, design in the universe, and second, that man is the *telos* of that design. Diderot and his fellow materialists rejected both. The universe is only nature, and nature knows only survival. 'In nature, all species devour each other; in society, all classes devour each other.'

Against this assault the optimist and the Christian set up a stout defence. We must now examine their arguments and counter-arguments. As Bayle may be said to have put the siege guns into firing position, so Leibniz set up the breast-works of the defence. His *Théodicée* (1710) was an answer to Bayle's *Dictionnaire*. But whereas Bayle's strategy remained operative throughout the years ahead, the defenders of the opposing camp found it necessary, about the middle of the century, to beat a hasty retreat from Leibniz's positions and to set up new defences.

Even as the materialists interpreted Spinoza's reasoning as substantiating a non-moral universe, so it is possible that Leibniz, by another interpretation, found in it the seed for his system of optimism. Spinoza had written that the eternal order of nature, 'wherein man is but a speck', is not that of human reason. Evil is an appearance resulting from our ignorance of 'the order and interdependence of nature as a whole'. What reason holds to be evil 'is not evil in respect to the laws of nature as a whole, but only in respect to the laws of our reason'.

Leibniz's system is based on the proposition that God is ultimately the sufficient reason of all particular things.

> Now, as in the Ideas of God there is an infinite number of possible universes, and as only one of them can be actual, there must be a sufficient reason for the choice of God, which leads him to decide upon one rather than another.
>
> And this reason can be found only in the *fitness* (*convenance*), or in the degrees of perfection, that these worlds possess, since each possible thing has the right to aspire to existence in proportion to the amount of perfection it contains in germ.
>
> Thus the actual existence of the best that wisdom makes known to God is due to this, that his goodness makes him choose it, and his power makes him produce it.

In this way Leibniz seeks to invalidate simultaneously three explanations of evil: the permissive doctrine of the scholastics, that God's will merely co-operates with ours; the Cartesian principle that God's will is the sole cause or agent in the universe; the Hobbesian thesis that God is a despotic or arbitrary power. Leibniz's optimism is entirely *a priori*, founded on 'sufficient reason' and the excellence of the cause, and cannot therefore be combated by experience. If the evil that individuals complain about were suppressed, this would no longer be the best of possible worlds, for 'all is linked'. God wills only the good; but when he compares goods, he can will them only as they are compatible and as, in unison, they produce the greatest good possible; and evil, precisely, is one of the conditions of this greatest good. Therefore, 'God wills the good antecedently, and the best consequently.' It is true that God is the real cause of everything positive in his creation, but none the less, he is not the cause of evil, which is a deficiency or limit. To put it differently, evil has no efficient cause, being only a privation, inherent in the condition or limits of the created.

The second great champion of optimism, and the most popular, was Alexander Pope. He was inspired by Shaftesbury through Bolingbroke, as well as by King and Leibniz. In particular, he favours Shaftesbury's

theory, that apparent evil is the result of our insufficient knowledge of the whole. Actually, Pope's optimism differed in many ways
from that of Leibniz. The English poet's system was in essence *a
posteriori*, founded on effects. 'What can we reason, but from what we
know?'—that is, from our own world. Furthermore Pope tends more
strongly to diminish, if not to deny, the reality of evil; in fact, the
harsh appearance of evil is dissolved into the reality of positive good.
'Whatever wrong we call, may, must be right, as relative to all.' Man
is 'perfect in his sphere'. 'All partial evil, universal good.' And of
course, 'Whatever is, is right.' God acts not by partial but by general
laws.

> All this dread ORDER break—for whom? for thee?
> Vile worm! Oh Madness! Pride! Impiety! (1, 257–258).

The optimism of Leibniz and Pope seems to have acted as an opiate
until the middle of the century. True, there was some resistance from
theologians who did not admit original sin as a necessary part of God's
best world, or who saw in optimism the denial of providence; and
there was a dawning realization that this 'optimism' consecrated our
ills *in perpetuum*. . . .

The orthodox, who even in the high tide of optimism had doubts
about the strategy of denying the reality of evil, openly denounced the
deistic optimists after the Lisbon earthquake. 'Fatal blindness!' cries
Formey. 'Does the infuriated lion who tears a traveller to pieces in the
vast forests of Libya seem to you then a good in the physical order?'
And are adultery, infamy, injustice, murder, rape, good? If evil is
prevalent in nature, should it not be so in guilty man? Should I say
that my suffering is only an increase in happiness? No, our suffering
is the very proof of God's continuing providence and justice. Other
apologists similarly abandon Leibnizianism and thus they free
God from responsibility on other grounds, which we shall shortly
examine.

As is well known, the Lisbon earthquake, which occurred in that
most Catholic of cities, on All Saints' Day, November 1, 1755, was a
'crise de conscience' for the eighteenth century. There was, it has been
seen, a growing, though a minority opposition to the Leibniz-Pope
types of optimism even before that event. In the preceding year the
Academy of Berlin had announced its essay contest for 1755, on the
distinction between Pope's 'Tout est bien' and 'the system of optimism or the choice of the best'. It was won by A. F. Reinhard whose

essay rejected optimism. The general good, argued the author, foreshadowing Voltaire's *Poème sur le désastre de Lisbonne*, is no consolation to me; suppose the general good required me to be forever unhappy?

After the shock of the earthquake, optimism crumbled, less, perhaps, because of the increased attacks upon it, than of its own dead weight. Actually, the sceptics and non-believers, even from the beginning, had levelled powerful assaults directly against the logic of the system of Leibniz and his followers. Bayle had early asserted that there must have been a better universe, in the infinity of possibles, than one which inevitably brought about the unhappiness of sensitive creatures. And if there was only one possible universe—then, what is God? Isn't there a Paradise? And wasn't there a Garden of Eden? Surely, these are better possibles! But if you take the opposite stand and argue that all possibles must be, then God had no freedom, had to choose evil and is its author. Thus runs Bayle's logic through all his writings, putting the faithful on a hook from which they struggled helplessly to free themselves. He had stated the case so well, that later *philosophes*, even after the Lisbon disaster, could do little but work the same substance into a new shape. One example, that of d'Alembert, will suffice. In the article 'Optimisme' in the *Encyclopédie* he opens up a frontal attack. Objecting to Leibniz's asseveration that the rape of Lucretia produced Rome's freedom and virtue, he inquires why virtues had to be produced by a crime. He, too, tries to show that it is impossible to reconcile optimism with God's freedom. Having posed the question, 'how many men kill each other in the best of possible worlds?' he goes on to demand why, if this is the best, God created it. In the article 'Fortuit', d'Alembert states bluntly that if God made the physical order, he is equally responsible for the moral order, even if contingent, that results from it.

As the earthquake renewed the problem of evil in acute form, demolishing the rampart of optimism on the one hand, and sharpening the pens of anti-Christians on the other, new defenders sprang into the breach. Shortly after the earthquake, the Academy of Rouen made it the subject of a prize essay (1757). The winner, Antoine Thomas, strives to demonstrate that the disaster was providential, a warning to make the impious tremble. Rousseau, in his reply to Voltaire's *Poème sur le désastre de Lisbonne* ('Lettre sur la Providence', August 18, 1756), contends that the fault is man's for living unnaturally in large cities—an argument also advanced by the abbé Pluquet the following year. Why should the quake have taken place in a desert, as Voltaire suggests?

Should the order of the world, counters Rousseau, echoing Pope, change to suit men's caprice?

The chorus of protests and counter attacks from believers and Christian apologists grew louder and stronger. It was as if there were a deepening realization that the fortress of optimism had fallen, and that unless they acted swiftly to close the breach, the *philosophes* would have a clear road to their three ultimate objectives: the dissolution of an ethical bond with God, 'secular morality', and deism or atheism. . . .

In view of all this perplexity, it is not surprising that a few writers, on both sides, threw up their hands and declared the problem insoluble. Saint-Martin and Delisle de Sales admitted this final *reductio*. Of course, this was also Bayle's 'conclusion', but doubtless not his ultimate intention.

It was also Voltaire's conclusion, and his sincere one. Probably no one, in the eighteenth century, was more greatly tormented by the problem of theodicy. This is to be expected, in view of his great uncertainties about providence. For many, the question was a problem in logic or polemics. Bayle enjoyed the logical game, the pleasure of tormenting his opponents. Voltaire felt a genuine metaphysical anguish. Once again, we can observe in the course of his thought the terrible perplexities that beset the eighteenth century humanist. Voltaire's Natural Law ethics needed a moral universe for its ground, in order to avoid the equivocality inherent in the word 'natural'. In his earlier years, he had preferred to shrug off the problem. A facile optimism reveals itself in the extrapolation from his own pleasurable life to a generalized belief in the preponderance of good and the benefits of progress (*Le Mondain*, 1736). By 1738 he is admitting the reality of evil and its equilibrium with good: 'Le malheur est partout, mais le bonheur aussi.' In the *Traité de métaphysique* (1734), he had worked hard to free God from the onus of evil. His attempt only forced him into a moral relativism that divorces God from all our human concepts. *Le monde comme il va* (1746) is still optimistic, though the doubts are more insistent. In *Zadig* (1747) we see him struggling, desperately now, to maintain his confidence. . . .

Although Voltaire was already cutting loose from optimism before the Lisbon earthquake, that event had a compelling and dramatic effect on him, provoking his *Poème sur le désastre de Lisbonne* (1756), which in turn aroused Rousseau to make an earnest and detailed rejoinder in his 'Lettre sur la Providence'. The central theme of the *Poème* is that providence may well exist, but it certainly ignores the well-being of a man on earth. He urges us to pity men, the eternal butt of 'useless pains'. Bayle's paradox has won:

> Direz-vous: C'est l'effet des éternelles lois
> Qui d'un Dieu libre et bon nécessitent le choix?

What has happened in Lisbon is not just. The Leibnizian optimist not only insults human pain, but condemns us to a despairing philosophy of necessity. 'We are then only wheels that make the great machine run; we are no more precious in God's eyes than the animals who devour us.'

Voltaire is torn. He asserts that man does not have an exceptional status, and yet condemns optimism because it implies that he does not. In the evolution of his thinking, he inclines more and more to a kind of materialistic naturalism in which he insists on making room for God, guarantor of value, shield against nihilism. As a believer in God and a humanist, he cannot join the atheistic materialist in his intellectual acceptance of evil in the universe. He opposes both philosophies (atheism, optimism) that accept evil, whence the impasse. At the same time he takes something from each: God from the optimist, an impersonal world-machine from the materialist; and the two are irreconcilable.

An Age of Crisis (Johns Hopkins Press, 1959), pp. 36-65.

14 The Crisis of Secularization

P. GAY

As men of letters at home in a world that was losing its Christian vocation, the *philosophes* felt this critical loss as a deep problem and solved it by reinterpreting and transforming their civilization. They made themselves the spokesmen for a revolutionary age in search of an interpreter.

The *philosophes* were men of letters. This is more than a phrase. It defines their vantage point, and eliminates the stale debate over their status as philosophers. As men of letters who took their craft seriously, they devoted to their writing an incessant care which is one of the secrets of their style. . . .

This devotion to the art of writing gave the *philosophes* the strength that comes from membership in a respectable guild; it gave them, for all their quarrels, common interests and a common vision. No matter how varied their concerns, they were men with a single career. . . . While they were literary men, they were neither bohemians nor alienated artists. While their view of their world was critical, and especially in religion, disruptive, they knew and loved the world they wished to change. Rousseau in some moods rejected it altogether, and asked for man's total regeneration, but it is significant that his fellow *philosophes* treated him as a madman long before his clinical symptoms became obvious. When they denounced civilization, they did so urbanely.

The *philosophes*, then, much as they wished to change it, were at home in their world. To divide the century into two sharply defined forces—the subversive *philosophes* against the orthodox—may be convenient and dramatic, but it is also much too simple. There were moments of crisis when two parties crystallized and Catholics squared off against unbelievers, but subtler and more pervasive than hostility were the ties that bound the *philosophes* to their society. They edited respectable magazines, flattered royal mistresses, wrote unexceptional entertainments, and held responsible posts.

Nor was their attachment to the existing order based solely on calculation: they shared with literate Christians a religious education, a love for the classics of Roman and French literature, and an affection for the pleasures of cultivated leisure. Seeking to distinguish themselves, they did not wish to abolish all distinctions. When they participated in politics, they often supported one orthodox party against another: Montesquieu, the *parlements* against the king; Voltaire, the king against the *parlements*. While they helped to prepare the way for the Jacobins, they were not Jacobins themselves.

Their attachment was strengthened by their association with a spectrum of would-be *philosophes*, half-*philosophes*, or Christians liberal enough to tolerate, or even to enjoy, men whose doctrines they rejected. Hangers-on, who basked in borrowed glory or second-hand notoriety, smuggled *philosophes*' letters, arranged for theatrical claques, and offered true friendship in a quarrelsome world. Strategically placed officials stood between *philosophes* and the severities of the law, and good Christians who dabbled in higher criticism or polite anticlericalism spread philosophic doctrines in respectable circles. In brief, the *philosophes* were deeply embedded in the texture of their society.

Yet this did not prevent them from being at war with it at the same time. The *philosophes* never developed a coherent political programme or even a consistent line of political tactics, but their polemics called for a France profoundly different from the country in which they lived—France after, not before, 1791. The regime could make concessions: boredom, a lost sense of purpose, could make many a bourgeois, priest, or aristocrat receptive to subversive propaganda. But aggressive deism or materialism, doctrines of the rule of law, complete toleration, and subordination of church to state—these tenets could not be assimilated by the old order. To neglect either side of their dual situation is to make the *philosophes* more revolutionary or more conservative than in fact they were.

This tension, which is yet not alienation, places not only the *philosophes* in their century, it places the century itself. To say that the eighteenth century was an age of contradictions, is to say nothing: all ages have this characteristic in common. We must be specific: eighteenth-century France was a Christian culture that was rapidly losing its Christian vocation without being fully aware of it. . . .

Most Frenchmen were wholly untouched by the Enlightenment and lived, as it were, in an earlier century. They believed in witches, applied spells, used home remedies long condemned by physicians, displayed a trust in authority long discarded by the educated, lived and died happily ignorant of the battles between Cartesians and Newtonians.

Yet for men sensitive or educated enough to be aware of intellectual currents, the eighteenth century was a time of turmoil. A whole complex of ideas and experiences, usually lumped together in the slippery word 'secularization', came together in the reign of Louis XV to haunt thinking men. The literature of travel offered the spectacle of happy and civilized non-Christian cultures; the demands of international politics forged secular rather than sectarian alliances; the growth of the European economy stimulated the desire for worldly goods; the great discoveries of science suggested the appalling possibility of a universe without God.

Secularization did not mean the death of religion. Eight Frenchmen out of ten—perhaps nine—were uncontaminated by scepticism. Even the businessman or artisan, who greatly benefited from advances in technology, rarely allowed them to affect his faith. Still, what Troeltsch has called the 'Church-directed civilization' was crumbling. Christians lived by the image of hierarchy: as God, his angels, and his creatures were arranged in an order of rank, so by analogy the skies, the family, law, society, the Church, were naturally hierarchical. Now, as natural scientists demonstrated that the hierarchies of terrestrial and celestial motion, or the spheres of the heavens, were absurd, other revolutionaries were exposing the absurdity of other hierarchies. . . .

Still, for all the impiety of the age, religion survived, and one reason for its survival was that the famous war between science and theology did not take place in the simple form familiar to us from the Whig Interpretation. The warfare began not between theology and science, but theology and some philosophical consequences drawn from science. It was not necessary to accept d'Alembert's positivism to be a good mathematician; or to be driven by Voltaire's anticlerical spleen to be a good Newtonian. Science, travel, politics, wealth, the great secularizing forces, did their work by indirection, as it were, behind the century's back. . . .

The crisis of secularization, then, was slower and subtler than we have been led to believe. It was also more pervasive. It was not confined to educated Christians, tormented by the startling conclusions of physicists. It was a problem for the *philosophes* themselves. It is not surprising that their anguish has received little attention—they covered it well with urbanity and noisy anticlericalism.

But anguish there was. The *philosophes* had two enemies: the institutions of Christianity and the idea of hierarchy. And they had two problems: God and the masses. Both the enemies and the problems were related and woven into the single task of rethinking their world. The old questions that Christianity had answered so fully for so many men and so many centuries, had to be asked anew: What—as Kant put it—what can I know? What ought I to do? What may I hope?

Science itself did not answer these questions. It only suggested—ever more insistently as the century went on—that the old answers were wrong. Now, the *philosophes* were products of Christian homes and Christian schools. If they became enemies of Christianity, they did so not from indifference or ignorance: they knew their Bible, their catechism, their Church Fathers, their apologetics. And they knew, because it had been drummed into them early, the fate that awaits heretics or atheists in the world to come. Their anticlerical humour therefore has the bitter intimacy of the family joke; to embrace materialism was an act of rejection.

The struggle of the *philosophes* was a struggle for freedom. They did not fully understand it, but to the extent that they did understand it, they knew their situation to be filled with terror and delight. They felt the anxiety and exhilaration of the explorer who stands before the unknown.

To use such existentialist language may seem like a rather portentous way of describing men noted for their sociability and frivolity. It is of course true that the *philosophes* did not suffer alone: they had the comforting company of elegant salons and of respectable philosophical forebears.

Yet even the supple Voltaire, who had been initiated into unbelief by fashionable teachers, was not free from the symptoms of this struggle. Much of his mockery was a weapon in a grim fight, and a device to keep up his own morale. Much of his philosophical rumination on free will reveals the persistence of a troublesome inner conflict.

It may not be fair to call to witness Rousseau, whose malaise was perpetual. But the shape of his suffering mirrors the suffering of his century. Nothing is more pathetic than Rousseau's attempt to rescue at least some comforting aspects of his universe from the icy blasts of Voltaire's cosmic pessimism. 'All the subtleties of metaphysics,' he wrote Voltaire, seeking to answer the poem on the Lisbon earthquake, 'will not make me doubt for a moment the immortality of the soul or a beneficent Providence. I feel it, I believe it, I want it, I hope for it, and I shall defend it to my last breath.' But the edifice of Rousseau's faith was flimsily built on illogical hope: the immortality of the soul and a beneficent Providence are articles of faith to which a Christian happily subscribes, but to which the deist, nourished on scientific scepticism, has no right.

Diderot, the most ebullient of *philosophes*, the freest and most inventive of spirits, was driven from position to position and haunted by doubts. Born into a family richly endowed with priests, of pious parents and with a fanatical brother, long toying with entering the priesthood, Diderot moved from Catholicism to theism, from theism to deism, from deism to scepticism, and from scepticism to atheism. But atheism, with its cold determinism, repelled him even though he accepted it as true; while Catholicism, with its colourful ceremony, moved him even though he rejected it as false. Writing to his mistress, Sophie Volland, he cursed the philosophy—his own—that reduced their love to a blind encounter of atoms. 'I am furious at being entangled in a confounded philosophy which my mind cannot refrain from approving and my heart from denying.'

The materialists of course claimed to be defiantly happy at being cosmic orphans. But the question—If God is dead, what is permitted?—was not a question calculated to make men sleep easy.

I am not simply arguing that the *philosophes* were less cheerful than they appeared in their social roles—most of us are. Nor that they suffered personal crises—philosophers, especially young philosophers, often do. I am arguing that the *philosophes'* anguish was related to the crisis in their Christian civilization; that (to use different language) whatever childhood experiences made them psychologically vulnerable in adult life, their obsessions, their self-questionings, their anxieties, were poured into their religious, moral, and political speculation.

The Party of Humanity (Weidenfeld and Nicolson, 1964), pp. 117–26.

VII

The Political Solution

In any assessment of the political ideas of this age, Rousseau is likely to play a leading role. Talmon (see pp. 111–13) leans heavily on the Rousseau of the *Social Contract* to illustrate his thesis that it was in the eighteenth century that totalitarian ideas were first elaborated. Gierke, on the other hand, although he saw Rousseau as moving towards the idea of a collective personality, still sketched him as basically an individualist, founding the state on the consent of individuals and building its collective person from the aggregation of individuals (see pp. 168–72). For Cassirer, Rousseau's originality lay in his linking of the problem of evil to social causes and political solutions. In absolving God (or nature) of blame for evil and attaching the guilt to society, Rousseau not only offers a new explanation of the theodicy problem but holds out hope of deliverance, not through God's mercy but through man's endeavours (see pp. 172–5). As can be seen from the quotation from Diderot's *Supplément au voyage de Bougainville*, Rousseau was not the only writer to forge this link (see pp. 60–61). Gay takes up and answers the charge, made most succinctly by Tocqueville, that the characteristic abstractness and unreality of Enlightenment political thought was due to the remoteness of the *philosophes* from practical affairs (see pp. 175–8).

15 Rousseau's Individualism

O. GIERKE

Meanwhile, in England and in France, the resuscitation of the theory of popular sovereignty had produced an attempt to give a more living content to the idea of Collective personality. Here the distinction between *societas aequalis* and *inaequalis* was dropped; and it thus became impossible to explain the development of Group-unity into a Being possessed of authority by referring that development to the institution of a Ruler who stood outside and above the community. If, under such conditions, there was to be any Group-unity which had the capacity of will and of action, and could be depicted as the 'Subject' of political authority, such unity had to be found not in a uniting Representative Ruler, but in the united community itself. The only question which then arose was whether it was possible—and if so, how it was possible—to raise the conception of Collective unity (the only conception possible as long as thought was confined to the limits of natural-law individualism) to the required degree of intensity.

In dealing with this problem, Locke marks but little advance. Although the community, on his own principles, is nothing but a partnership of individuals who remain individuals, he yet makes it also, at the same time, a single body. His treatment of the majority-principle is a good illustration of his method. On the one hand, he seeks to derive it from the nature of the community as a single body. All bodies, he argues, must be moved by a single power in a single way; in the body politic, the only motive power discoverable is the superior power possessed by the majority; therefore the identification of majority-will with the will of the whole is a consequence of the Law of Nature and Reason. On the other hand, and in the same breath [recurring to the idea of partnership], he thinks it necessary to suppose a contractual agreement of all individuals to submit to the future resolutions of a majority, and he makes this agreement the legal basis of the validity of such resolutions.

Rousseau occupied himself far more seriously with the problem of raising Collective unity to the dignity of a living and authoritative Group-person. It was a problem which was particularly pressing for him, because he rejected absolutely any idea of Representative unity. He asserts again and again that the social contract produces a moral body equipped with authority over its members; that such a body, like the natural body, is a single and indivisible whole; and that it possesses an Ego, a life, a will of its own. He makes this real Group-being, under the name and style of a 'moral person', the one and only Sovereign, which not only stands on a level with actual individuals in all its external relations, but is also the genuine 'Subject' of political authority internally. But vigorously as he sought to depict the substantive existence of this sovereign Group-person, Rousseau was unable to escape from the trammels of a view which made it, after all, only a sum of individuals united in a single aggregate. But how could a contract between individuals conceivably produce anything which was not itself a mere matter of individuals? Rousseau attempts to meet the difficulty. He argues that the associated individual wills blend together in a general will (*volonté générale*), which is no longer the will of all (*volonté de tous*). But all the dialectical arts which he uses in order to prove that the general will is different from the will of all fail to turn it into a genuine common will. In the last resort the whole distinction comes to this— that the will of all is the sum of individual wills, including all their actual variations from one another, while the general will is to be found by adding the concordant motives of individual wills, and excluding all their dissonances. The innate character of this general will is not even sufficient to produce the principle of majority-rule; and if majority-rule is to be substituted for it, it must be stipulated for in an agreement —though it is only fair to add that Rousseau regards such an agreement as indispensable. The supposed general will is thus, after all, no more than an average of individual wills, to be found by the use of a ready-reckoner. Only a miracle can enable it to show the higher qualities which Rousseau poetically credits it with possessing.

[Just as the general will stays at the level of an average of individual wills, so] the sovereign Group-person never rises beyond the sum total of individuals who constitute the society at any given time. The same persons who are governed, in their capacity of subjects, also constitute the sovereign in their other capacity of citizens. Each is, in part, the joint-owner of a sovereign authority to which, at the same time, the whole of himself is subject.[1] Corresponding to this double position [of subject and citizen], in virtue of which the individual can contract with himself and owe obedience to himself, there is a double series of obligations which the social contract creates for the individual. But while the individual thus incurs obligations, it is inconceivable that the sovereign community should be bound, either by the social contract itself, or by any other sort of law. It can undertake obligations, in the same way as an individual, in reference to third parties: it can never oblige itself, as a Whole, to any of its own members. By its very nature,[2] this sovereign moral person manifests itself totally, and manifests itself exclusively, in

---

[1] Compare the epigram of a French writer: 'The modern Frenchman looks with pride at his face in the glass as he shaves in the morning, remembering that he is the thirty millionth part of a tyrant, and forgetting that he is the whole of a slave.'

[2] By its very nature—as being one with *all* its members, from whom it can never separate itself, even for the purpose of obliging itself.

the assembly of all. It manifests itself totally in that assembly, in the sense of being so identical with it that each new assembly cancels the whole of the previous political and legal situation; and each new assembly, therefore, unless it prefers an alteration of that situation, or a modification of it, has to give it the validity which it would otherwise lack by an act of express or tacit confirmation. [As it manifests itself totally in the assembly, so also the Sovereign manifests itself exclusively in that body.] In it, and in it alone, can the Sovereign show itself a being which acts and wills. Any form of 'Representation' of the sovereign Collective being is incompatible with the very conception of that being. The moral person is so entirely bound up with a visible aggregation of individuals, that no idea of any 'Organ', through which the invisible but living unity of a social body attains an active expression, can ever possibly emerge.

But in spite of his theory of the primary assembly, Rousseau is forced to provide some sort of permanent organization for the community, and to fill in some way the void which he has created by abolishing the Representative unity involved in the existence of a Ruler. He therefore devises an ingenious system by which the sovereign moral person creates, in the shape of an administrative body (*gouvernement*), a second moral person—subservient to itself, but yet possessing a life of its own; acting with a delegated and dependent authority, but acting none the less. But this secondary moral person turns out, once more, to be only a Collective unity, composed of individuals, and never transcending the individuals who compose it.

The theory of Rousseau exercised a great influence on the natural-law theory of Group-personality; but even in France, where it passed into the programme of the Revolution, it was considerably modified, mainly in the direction of bringing it more within the bounds of political possibility. It was Sieyès who, more than any other writer, gave to Rousseau's theory the popular form in which it long continued to inspire the political doctrines of Radicalism. Like Rousseau, he identified the moral personality of the social body with the sum of its individual members, regarded as a single aggregate; like him, he identified the common will with the will of all; like him, again, he identified the will of all with the will of the majority, in virtue of an agreement of all supposed to have been made for that purpose. But Sieyès restored the idea of Representation which Rousseau had rejected; and he therefore regarded a Collective unity as not only operative in a primary assembly of all its members, but also willing and acting through its appointed representatives. He was thus able to eliminate from the State the idea of a separate moral personality of the Government, which had been introduced by Rousseau—substituting, in its place, a scheme by which a variety of different bodies represented the sovereign community.

Natural Law and the Theory of Society (Beacon Press, 1960), pp. 128–31.

16 Rousseau and the Problem of Evil

E. CASSIRER

Rousseau's real originality and significance lie in an entirely different sphere; it is not the problem of God but the problem of law and society which occupies all his thinking. But in this respect he establishes a new relation and welds a new connecting-link. Rousseau is the first to carry this problem beyond the sphere of individual human existence and to turn it expressly towards the problem of society. In society Rousseau believed he had found the decisive feature of the meaning of human existence, of human happiness or misery. Such was the conclusion he derived from his study and criticism of political and social institutions. In the *Confessions* he says of himself: 'I saw that everything depended basically on political science, and that, no matter how one views the problem, every people is just what its government makes it. The great question of the best possible form of government seemed to lead me back to the other question: "What form of government is most suited to produce a nation which is virtuous, enlightened, wise—in short, in the highest sense of the word, as perfect as possible?" ' A new norm for human existence appears here; instead of the mere desire for happiness, the idea of law and social justice is made the standard by which human existence is to be measured and tested. At first the application of this standard leads Rousseau to a completely negative decision. All the assets which mankind believes it has acquired in the course of its development —all the treasures of knowledge, of art, of increased refinement and enjoyment of life—vanish before Rousseau's inexorable criticism. Far from having given life new value and substance, these supposed benefits have drawn it farther and farther away from its source until they have finally robbed it of its real meaning. In his presentation of the traditional and conventional forms of life and of human existence in

society Rousseau to a surprising degree finds himself in agreement with
Pascal. He is the first thinker in the eighteenth century to take Pascal's
accusation against man seriously and to feel its full force. Instead of
softening it, instead of attributing it to the self-torturing mood of a
brooding misanthropist, as Voltaire had done, Rousseau grasps its cardinal point. The description of the greatness and misery of man which
occurs in Pascal's *Thoughts* is revived in Rousseau's early writings, in
his prize essay on the arts and sciences, and in his *Discourse on Inequality*.
Amid the dazzling lustre with which civilization has adorned the life
of man Rousseau, like Pascal, sees only illusion and tinsel. Rousseau,
too, insists that all this wealth is calculated only to blind man to his own
inner poverty. Man takes refuge in society, in a variety of activities and
diversions only because he cannot bear his own thoughts and the sight
of himself. All this restless and aimless activity arises from his fear of
quiet; for if he were to stop for only a single moment to reflect upon
his own condition, he would fall prey to the deepest and most hopeless
despair. Regarding the forces which, in the present state of society, tend
to bring individuals together, Rousseau entertains the same opinion as
Pascal. He stresses repeatedly that there is no original moral impulse, no
desire for community in its true sense in the present state of society, nor
any natural sympathy uniting one man to another. All social ties are
based on mere illusions. Egotism and vanity, the impulse to dominate
and to impress others; such are the real bonds that hold society together. 'Just a lacquer of words everywhere, just a mad scramble for a
happiness which exists only in appearance. Nobody is concerned with
reality any more; all suppose it to lie in illusion. They drift along
through life as slaves of self-love; not in order to live, but in order to
make others believed they have lived.'

Rousseau thus admits all the premises on which Pascal had based his
reasoning. He undertakes no embellishment or attenuation; like Pascal
he depicts the present state of mankind as one of extreme decadence.
But although Rousseau recognizes the phenomenon on which Pascal
bases his argument, he stoutly rejects the interpretation which Pascal's
mysticism and religious metaphysics had offered for it. Rousseau's
feeling and thinking both rebel against Pascal's hypothesis of an original
perversion of the human will. The idea of the fall of man has lost all its
force and validity for Rousseau. On this point he opposed orthodoxy
no less severely and radically than did Voltaire and the French Encyclopaedists. It was indeed this dogma which brought about his irreconcilable conflict and final break with the teachings of the Church. In its

judgment concerning Rousseau's writings the Church itself stresses this central point at once clearly and confidently as the really decisive problem. The mandate in which Christophe de Beaumont, archbishop of Paris, condemns *Émile* points out that Rousseau's thesis that the first impulses of human nature are always innocent and good stands in sharpest conflict with all the doctrines of the Bible and the Church concerning the nature of man. But Rousseau himself now faces a dilemma from which there seems to be no escape. If he admits the fact of human degeneration, if he indeed repeatedly insists on this fact and paints it out in the darkest colours, how can he escape the cause of degeneration, how evade the conclusion of radical evil? Rousseau extricates himself from this dilemma by introducing at this point his doctrine of nature and the 'state of nature'. Every time we pronounce judgment on man, we must distinguish most carefully as to whether our statement applies to 'natural man' (*l'homme naturel*) or to 'civilized man' (*l'homme artificiel*). Whereas Pascal had explained the insoluble contradictions of human nature by asserting that, metaphysically considered, man has a twofold nature, Rousseau on the other hand finds this conflict in human nature in the midst of empirical existence and development. This development had indeed compelled man to adopt a compulsory form of society, thus exposing him to all moral evils; it had fostered in him all the vices of vanity, arrogance, and boundless greed for power. Rousseau's *Émile* begins with the words: 'All is well when it leaves the hands of the Creator of things; all degenerates in the hands of man.' Thus God is condoned and guilt for all evil is attributed to man. But since guilt belongs to this world, not to the world beyond; since it does not exist before the empirical, historical existence of mankind, but arises out of this existence, we must therefore seek redemption solely in this world. No help from above can bring us deliverance. We must bring it about ourselves and be answerable for it. With this conclusion Rousseau finds the new approach to the problem of evil which he follows in his political writings undeviatingly to its logical consequences. Rousseau's ethical and political theory places responsibility where it had never been looked for prior to his time. Its historical significance and systematic value lie in the fact that it creates a new subject of 'imputability'. This subject is not individual man but society. The individual as such, as he comes from nature's workshop, is still without the pale of good and evil. He follows his natural instinct of self-preservation, and he is governed by his 'self-love' (*amour de soi*); but this self-love has not yet degenerated into 'selfish love' (*amour propre*) whose only satisfaction lies in the subjection of others to its will. Society alone is responsible for this kind of selfish love. It is such egotism which causes man to turn tyrant against nature and even against himself. It awakens in him wants and passions which natural man knew nothing of, and it also provides him with the new means with which he can gratify these desires and passions without restraint. Eagerness to be talked of and the passion to distinguish ourselves before others, prevent us from knowing ourselves and lure us, so to speak, out of ourselves. But is this self-estrangement grounded in the nature of every society? Is not a truly human community conceivable which no longer depends on these motives of power, greed, and vanity, but which is entirely based on a law recognized as inwardly binding and necessary? Such is the question which Rousseau now raises and which he attempts to answer in his *Social Contract*. When the compulsory form of society, which has hitherto prevailed, falls and is replaced by a new form of political and ethical community— a community in which every member, instead of being subjected to the arbitrary will of others, obeys only the general will which he recognizes and acknowledges as his own—then the hour of deliverance has arrived. But it is futile to expect this deliverance from without. No God can bring it about for us; man must rather become his own deliverer and in the ethical sense his own creator. Society heretofore has inflicted the deepest wounds on mankind; yet it is society too which through a transformation and reformation can and should heal these wounds. Such is Rousseau's solution of the problem of theodicy in his philosophy of law. And he has in fact placed this problem on an entirely new footing, removing it from the sphere of metaphysics and making it the focal point of ethics and politics.

The Philosophy of the Enlightenment (Beacon Press, 1951), pp. 153–8.

17 Abstract, Literary Politics

P. GAY

Perhaps the boldest and certainly the most influential attempt to deny Voltaire the quality of political realism was undertaken by Tocqueville in the middle of the nineteenth century. In *L'Ancien régime et la révolution française*, Tocqueville depicted French writers as keenly interested and wholly unschooled in practical questions: they dealt with politics 'casually, even, one might say, toyed with them. But all took notice of them in one way or another. This kind of abstract, literary politics found its way, in varying proportions, into all the writings of the day.' As abstract, literary political thinkers, whatever their divergences of opinion, the philosophes unanimously extolled a society based on 'simple, elementary rules deriving from the exercise of the human reason and natural law'. All they adored were reason and intellect—their own. Such a political philosophy was the height of Utopianism and impiety, but it was the only philosophy available to them: 'Their very way of living led these writers to indulge in abstract theories and generalizations regarding the nature of government, and to place a blind confidence in these. For living as they did, quite out of touch with practical politics, they lacked the experience which might have tempered their enthusiasms . . . they had little acquaintance with the realities of public life, which, indeed, was *terra incognita* to them.'

Thus Tocqueville; Jacob Burckhardt went further, suggesting that the philosophes did not even take an interest in politics: 'In the Age of Reason, when the state seemed unchanged, it was actually cast into the shade by people who did not care to discuss the events of the day, but ruled the world as philosophes—a Voltaire, a Rousseau, etc. . . . . The State was subjected to the most powerful action of thought, of philosophical abstraction. . . .'

This estimate, a notable contribution to the Voltaire legend, lends authority to the widespread notion that Voltaire supported, perfected, or perhaps even invented 'enlightened despotism'. This abstract, literary conception of the omnipotent ruler, who governs an obedient people by the sole light of reason and under the guidance of his court philosophe, is precisely the Utopian political philosophy—contemptuous of tradition and existing institutions, oblivious to the power of irrationality—to be expected from an old child, a man 'quite out of touch with practical politics'.

But the Voltaire legend, which inevitably leads to such unjust oversimplifications, is wholly untenable. That Voltaire was excitable, that he changed his mind, that he contradicted himself—all this no student of his writings and his correspondence will deny. He lived too long, wrote too much, expressed opinions too casually, participated in affairs too vividly not to be on opposite sides of various questions at different times. But it does not follow that his political philosophy was a 'chaos of clear ideas', as Émile Faguet characterized it in an epigram that has become only too familiar; it does not follow that he was incapable of practical thought, addicted to abstract ideas, fundamentally unserious. These charges are all the more grave for being repeated so often and for being so untrue. The variety of his interests and the shifts in his political opinions sprang not from flightiness but from an empiricist's temper, not from detachment but from a deep engagement with reality. When he talked nonsense about politics, he did so because he was remote from the events on which he was commenting so rashly. When he knew what he was talking about, when he observed events, talked to politicians, studied documents, as he did in England, France, and Geneva, his political judgments were cool and penetrating, hardheaded and practical.

In fact, Voltaire and his fellow philosophes were closer to affairs than Tocqueville asserts: d'Argenson was intendant, ambassador and foreign minister; Turgot was intendant and finance minister; Quesnay was the king's physician and close to the makers of policy; Montesquieu and Hénault were prominent magistrates, Helvétius held a position at court and was a tax farmer; Rousseau, who was on the edges of politics in France, was at the centre of politics in Geneva, and while it can be argued that his *Discours sur l'inégalité* and the *Contrat social* are abstract, theoretical works, his political writings on Geneva, Poland, and Corsica display the tough-minded common sense of a man in touch with reality. And Voltaire spent much of his life with diplomats, ministers, intendants, politicians, magistrates and courtiers; he wrote dispatches for d'Argenson, went to Prussia on a diplomatic mission, corresponded with ministers like Choiseul and Turgot and powerful judges like Hénault, was intimate with Bolingbroke in England and with the political leaders of Geneva, and kept in touch with the controversies of his day.

But Voltaire was the symbol of his age, and it is the fate of symbols to be exploited rather than to be understood. Writers seeking to strike at the Enlightenment through him saw only what they wanted to see. The German *Stürmer und Dränger* repudiated Voltaire as a son repudiates his father to gain maturity. German Augustans—earnestly in search of their German past, energetically dedicated to the creation of a German literature, humourlessly insistent upon the superiority of the German character—found it necessary to depict Voltaire as the incarnation of French irreverence, superficiality, and frivolity. The antirevolutionary tradition in France, from Chateaubriand to Taine, from de Maistre to Faguet, evolved an image of Voltaire the brilliant, impious conspirator, subverting the Old Regime which had deserved to survive for all its flaws. Tocqueville and Taine conceded that its taxes had been inequitable, its privileges infuriating, and its critics often right, but they implied that men of practical sense would have tried to preserve and reform it. Instead, the philosophes, addicted to the geometric, classical spirit, feverishly and irresponsibly destroyed it. Such lighthearted *littérateurs* do not understand the meaning of politics. . . .

There are two ways of being unpolitical: to think that politics can do everything, and to think that politics can do nothing. The first leads to Utopianism and fanaticism, the second to Epicureanism and apathy; yet, despite their opposite effects, both are symptoms of the same disease, a failure of realistic vision. The makers of the legend have freely attributed both symptoms to Voltaire—cannot a flighty poet easily move from fanaticism to apathy? He has been charged with overestimating the efficacy of politics, believing that all unhappiness can be cured and all social problems solved, and at the same time wanting to dissolve politics into ethics, wishing to achieve impossible goals by the mere application of reason without the use of force.

This legend does violence to the truth. Voltaire accepted limitations on political action; he agreed with the Machiavellians that private and public spheres are separate and that political power has imperatives of its own. But he rejected a philosophy that free political actions from criticism and permits statesmen to act ruthlessly, faithlessly, brutally, with the excuse that power is demonic and that necessity knows no law. Far from seeking to make politics a panacea or from dissolving it in ethics, Voltaire sought to humanize it.

Voltaire's Politics (Princeton University Press, 1959), pp. 7–14.

VIII

Progress and History

In what ways was the idea of progress related to the faith in science? This is a question that Frankel attempts to answer by distinguishing two influences, that of the Cartesian view of science which envisaged the scientific method as achieving knowledge of absolute, unprovisional truths, and that of Pascal (or, as Frankel might more persuasively have said, Newton) for whom the scientific method was a cumulative and self-correcting process leading to provisional truths which in turn were subject to testing and revision by the method itself. The Cartesian view was profoundly ahistorical, for it was bound to pose stark alternatives of darkness and light, to see the new method (as Descartes himself did) as flowing from a sudden revelation and thus to paint history as the sorry and unmitigated record of vice and error. On the other view, since science is self-correcting, the past and the future present themselves as gradually moving from darkness to light in a steady, unbroken progression. Vyverberg does not deny the development of an idea of progress in the eighteenth century, but he does seek to show that, even amongst the *philosophes* themselves, this was not a postulate that went unquestioned (see pp. 185–6).

Collingwood is quoted as a typical statement of the charge that the Enlightenment lacked any real historical insight and that, obsessed by its philosophic aims and convinced of its own rationality, it was unable to attain that modesty and disinterestedness which makes possible the understanding in all its uniqueness of the remote past (see pp. 187–9). Trevor-Roper, an historian himself rather than a philosopher of history, gives a more balanced assessment of the achievements of the age of Hume, Voltaire, Robertson and Gibbon (see pp. 189–92).

18 The Roots of the Idea of Progress

C. FRANKEL

Unlike those in an industrial age whose belief in progress rested on the physical powers of science, the *philosophes* were primarily interested in the immediate moral implications of the scientific enterprise. Their vision of science was essentially that for which Descartes supplied the major impulse: they were interested in science as Method, as a systematic procedure for distinguishing the true from the false. Science was Enlightenment, the questioning and illumination of all beliefs by the individual's 'natural light'. For the *philosophes* as for Descartes, Method was not simply a limited technique to be used only on specified occasions, but a universal instrument of criticism and a new morality of action, something to be assimilated into the daily habits of the individual and society. As Descartes had said, each and every advance in science was to be esteemed not so much for its own sake as for its contribution to the perfecting of Method.

Within this broad view, however, different conceptions of the nature of science and enlightenment were possible. As we have seen, two divergent theories of progress were really present in the works of the *philosophes*, and a brief summary may help us to bring their differences into focus and to consider the issues between them.

The primary source of the first theory of progress lies in Descartes. While Descartes had made it plain that the choice of his Method was the choice of a way of behaving, he had also made it plain that the justification of this Method lay not only in its fruits, though these were great, but in the unprovisional truth of the principles on which it was based. Unless he were to involve himself in a logical circle, Descartes could not use his mathematical method to discover or establish these principles: rather, these principles provided an antecedent guarantee that his mathematical method was the exclusive agency of intellectual and moral progress. Descartes fixed the conviction upon later generations that the methods of science require an external guarantee. His Method was more than simply the orderly analysis of problems into their simple elements, or the systematic application of mathematics to all spheres: it was these techniques plus the metaphysical propositions that made their conclusions absolute and exclusive.

It was in this way that the conception of science and enlightenment came to connote not only an habitual attitude of critical inquiry but a set of absolute beliefs upon which inquiry and action must rest, and which are not themselves modifiable by further inquiry. While the *philosophes* employed the empiricist language of Locke, their empiricism remained essentially Cartesian and rationalistic, retaining the conviction that the particular grammar in terms of which they chose to express their experience was the only grammar nature used. The *philosophes* tended to think of reason and enlightenment as a system of simple, indubitable, and eternal truths, and through their metaphysical 'experimental physics of the soul' they attempted to provide an external framework for the interpretation of human inquiry and progress.

The consequence was a theory of progress which, paradoxically, recapitulated in a different language the main features of the theological interpretation of history which the *philosophes* were combating. The emergence of science became either the product of a revelation, a sudden discovery without historical antecedents, and carrying its own certificate of validity, or it became the culmination of a process in which all evil was not really or finally evil, and all errors were necessary steps in the improvement of mankind. The harmonious order of nature emerged as a thinner version of Providence.

This interpretation of the conclusions of science apart from its selective methods, and in terms of the metaphysical belief in a necessary order of reason, was responsible for the dualistic elements in the theories of progress developed by the *philosophes*. For what did not meet the standards of reason, what, for example, did not follow the natural, reasonable order of the development of ideas out of sensations, had to be assigned to the sphere of accident and disorder. Thus, d'Alembert, following suggestions in Condillac, distinguished between the 'metaphysical' account of progress, which exhibited the 'necessary', and therefore intelligible, itinerary of 'the isolated spirit', and the 'historical' account of the succession of ideas, which simply recapitulated the accidental order in which ideas had happened to succeed one another. This was an order which was distorted by the accident of social organization and the influence of the past. The actual history of progress was thus separated from the eternal principles that made progress natural and necessary.

This separation of philosophy and reason from history and experience was, of course, an extraordinarily effective weapon when it was used, for example by Voltaire, to show that history was an almost unbroken lapse from reason, and that there was, despite high-sounding rationalizations and claims to universality, an inevitable element of irrational preference or local prejudice in any human judgment. The idea of reason gave the histories written during the Enlightenment a further philosophic and critical import. The philosopher-historians of the Enlightenment, whose appeal to reason expressed a concern to extricate the underlying unity from the variety of details, were convinced that a mere narrative of the order in which individual events had followed one another explained nothing, and, indeed, did not quite do what it pretended to be doing. The *philosophes* were acutely conscious of the role of selection in the writing of histories, both in those of their opponents and in their own, and they felt that no history could in fact be merely a chronicle, but had to involve some general principles of selection. If it was to explain anything, history had to be a phase of science and philosophy: it had to employ general laws, and be illuminated by insight into constant factors in human conduct and perennial moral truths.

It was, however, the very interpretation of reason as a set of metaphysical and eternal truths which prevented the integration of philosophy and history, and introduced the paradoxes into the *philosophes'* theories of progress. Reason was formulated in terms which were explicitly disengaged from the historical process itself. A metaphysical psychology and theory of natural rights described what would have happened had not history, change, and the contingent intervened. Given this theory, the issue for the *philosophes* was not to explain how progress had come about, but, indeed, why it had not come about.

The idea of reason as a set of unassailable metaphysical truths produced a paradoxical theory of progress because it interpreted scientific criticism and inquiry as instruments in the realization of ideals or goals that were not themselves subject to further inquiry or parts of a progressive process. The consequence was that ends and means were separated, ends being assigned to a realm of necessity, while means were left in the realm of the contingent. The relation between ends and means thus became purely mechanical. The connection between any particular means and a given end was interpreted as only adventitious and temporary: in another situation, another means might accomplish the same end. The mechanistic interpretation of the relation of means and ends, which holds that a means may produce a given end without itself being among the actual ingredients present in the outcome, is thus the expression of a kind of surreptitious supernaturalism in which the end is in the last analysis guaranteed, while the particular means employed can be blamed on the accidents of history. So even the crimes and follies of the past might lead to the reign of reason, nature and humanity.

There was present in the theories of the *philosophes*, however, the suggestion of a view that offered an alternative to these paradoxes. In Rousseau's protests against the narrowness of the empiricist views of human experience, in Diderot's attacks upon mechanistic interpretations of matter and thought, and in his biological and evolutionary insights, paths were broken that moved beyond the emphasis of rationalist empiricism on the necessity for predetermined goals and an antecedent metaphysical guarantee. And there ran through the reflections of many of the *philosophes* the recognition, exemplified by Pascal, that the method of science was unique among intellectual authorities in that it was a cumulative and self-corrective process. When the conditions and impact of this method were explored and dramatized by the philosopher-historians, the conception of social progress as the extension of the habit of free inquiry was developed.

To many there is, of course, something unsatisfactory in this dismissal of the necessity for a higher metaphysical or moral justification of science. If the conclusions reached by scientific method are to be checked only by other conclusions reached by the same method, are we not involved in a logical circle? How do we know that the method itself is reliable? It is only from the point of view of the Cartesian demand for certainty and finality, however, that such questions must be answered by demonstrating that science rests on absolutely firm foundations. The Cartesian proof that science was a progressive agency had been that scientific knowledge was progressive because its absolute reliability had been established on higher grounds. In contrast, what was implied in this second view of science was that scientific knowledge was reliable because it was indefinitely progressive. Scientific knowledge was progressive not because it rested on unprovisionally true premises, but precisely because the truths it established were all provisional, the means to new investigations, and subject to test and enlargement by further inquiry.

To the contemporary 'problem' of the so-called 'irresponsibility' of science a similar answer may be made. Free inquiry becomes servile and irresponsible only when it is subordinated to external goals which are not themselves held to be within its domain. Inquiry does not 'invent' values; it must find them where they are, in custom, tradition, the arts, and creative experience. But it is only the introduction of the progressive methods of organized inquiry that makes the moralities that grow out of these values progressive. In short, from the point of view of this interpretation of the relation of science to progress, scientific method does not need the justification of a higher morality: it is our moralities which require the kind of integrated growth which is exemplified where the method of science is employed.

The general disrepute into which the dogma of necessary progress has fallen has cast a cloud not only over those elements in the beliefs of the *philosophes* which may be defensible, but over the liberal philosophy in which the belief in human betterment through the use of intelligence is a central part. The scientists and the humanist are today held to be at odds, the one irresponsible, the other impotent. There are those who hold that the belief in the powers of intelligence shows a failure in imagination, or loss of a 'tragic sense of life', and the man who holds that scientific method provides the most reliable way of obtaining truths and controlling conduct may find himself accused of 'scientism', or even of 'rationalism'.

Under these circumstances, it is worth remembering that the *philosophes* thought that reason and humanity were one. Undoubtedly, their rationalism was sometimes dogmatic and shallow, though not so often as is sometimes alleged. But where they failed it was essentially a failure of imagination, and this failure of imagination was not due to their attachment to science, but to a metaphysical theory which exalted the categories of physics into the exclusive properties of nature, and told them beforehand the kind of thing they could expect to find, and the properties of things they would have to reject as secondary and illusory. The separation of science and humanism is a consequence of this metaphysics. But the *philosophes* also succeeded in transcending this rigid idea of reason. They brought science and humanism together by showing that the values incorporated into the methods of reason were also the values that were basic if the pursuit of any other values was to be stabilized and controlled. It was the *philosophes* who laid the foundations for the conviction that the moral significance of science lies in the opportunity its methods present to develop responsible and informed uses of social power, and they are largely responsible for the liberal faith that freedom of thought, equality, and co-operative inquiry are ingredients of any progressive morality.

The Faith of Reason (King's Crown Press, Columbia University, 1948), pp. 153–8.

19 Historical Pessimism

H. VYVERBERG

At first glance this work might seem a laboured and sustained paradox. The belief in progress has long been considered the culmination of eighteenth century thought, and any attack upon this proposition will rightly be regarded with distrust. Yet the time for a re-examination of the facts is overdue. What follows in these pages is a sketch, a suggestion, of such a reconsideration—an attempt not only to weigh with special caution the historical philosophies of the French Enlightenment, but also to examine the substructure of thought which underlay them and which often led directly, perhaps inevitably, not to a belief in human progress but to historical pessimism.

It is clear that the eighteenth century saw the development of an idea of progress; clearly, too, there were writers and men of action who generously transformed idea into belief. This study does not, certainly, seek to deny these facts. But how widespread was this belief? Which intellectual factions resisted or ignored the optimistic trend, and why? What disturbing uncertainties and intellectual reservations entered the minds of even the master builders of the Enlightenment as they proposed to draw the blueprints of the future? These questions demand serious study, though doubtless they will never be answered to the satisfaction of all. If, for the moment, a few misconceptions concerning the Enlightenment can be exposed, if here and there an emphasis is significantly shifted, the historian may be permitted to feel that a truer understanding of one vital aspect of the past has been achieved.

The central contention of the present study is simply this: that a belief in progress was neither the exclusive focus nor the one logical consummation of Enlightened French philosophy, and that historical pessimism too had its roots deep in the 'philosophical' movement itself. The eighteenth century saw a rich proliferation of intellectual currents, and within this growth lay potentialities immensely dangerous to that rationalistic-optimistic synthesis which too often is assumed to have been the ultimate contribution of the century. The thought of the Enlightenment was neither as disembodied and visionary, nor as simple or oversimplified, as it was once imagined, and as it is pictured now and again in our own day.

If, as I believe, the prevalence and the significance of the eighteenth century belief in progress have been overrated, several roads to misinterpretation are evident. There have been, for example, few thinkers indeed in any age who have not cherished a hope for progress according to their own lights; what has not been fully recognized by historians of the Enlightenment is that the hope for progress need not involve a firm belief in the realization of that progress. In this period, as in others, the most fervent expression of an ideal might be accompanied by scepticism as to its practicality and even its final validity. Man is sometimes less consistent than might be concluded from a rationalistic view of human nature.

Often, in fact, the thinkers of the Enlightenment saw the historical movement of mankind as irregular or cyclical, and often the historian, in his zeal for tracing the development of progressionist theory, has slighted or wholly ignored these significant conceptions of cultural decline. Other thinkers of the period were openly hostile to the idea of progress as then conceived, while still others were simply indifferent to man's progressive development; both groups have been almost entirely neglected by the historian. Moreover, it is commonly assumed, when these supposedly atypical trends are noted at all, that they are part of the negligible clerical, reactionary thought of the eighteenth century. Closer examination, however, reveals not only the utter divergence of historical philosophies among the religious writers of the time, but also the presence of historical pessimism in the thought of the *philosophes* themselves.

'Historical pessimism'—the term admittedly lacks precision, yet it must serve here for lack of a better. It is applied in this study to the acceptance, as realities, of one or more of three historical processes: decadence, cycles, and flux. By the three concepts indicated here, and by the idea of progress, mankind has sought to explain or to describe its temporal existence, and to predict its future as well. But the movement of history is complex and its interpretation offers countless variations; neither the Enlightenment nor any other period of Western thought has shown unanimity in its view of historical change.

Historical Pessimism in the French Enlightenment (University Press, 1958), pp. 1–3.

20 The Unhistorical Enlightenment

R. G. COLLINGWOOD

Hume, in his historical work, and his slightly older contemporary Voltaire stand at the head of a new school of historical thought. Their work and that of their followers may be defined as the historiography of the Enlightenment. By the Enlightenment, *Aufklärung*, is meant that endeavour, so characteristic of the early eighteenth century, to secularize every department of human life and thought. It was a revolt not only against the power of institutional religion but against religion as such. Voltaire regarded himself as the leader of a crusade against Christianity, fighting under the motto *Écrasez l'infâme*, where *l'infâme* meant superstition, religion considered as a function of what was backward and barbarous in human life. The philosophical theory underlying this movement was that certain forms of mental activity are primitive forms, destined to perish when mind arrives at maturity. According to Vico, poetry is the natural mode in which the savage or childish mind expresses itself; the sublimest poetry, he maintains, is the poetry of barbarous or heroic ages, the poetry of Homer or Dante; as man develops, reason prevails over imagination and passion, and poetry is displaced by prose. Intermediately between the poetic or purely imaginative way of presenting its experience to itself, and the prosaic or purely rational, Vico placed a third, the mythical or semi-imaginative. This is the stage of development which puts upon the whole of experience a religious interpretation. Thus Vico thinks of art, religion, and philosophy as three different ways in which the human mind expresses or formulates to itself its whole experience. They cannot live peaceably side by side; their relation to each other is one of dialectical succession in a definite order. It follows that a religious attitude towards life is destined to be superseded by a rational or philosophical one.

No such theory was consciously formulated either by Voltaire or by Hume. But had such a theory been brought to their notice, they might have accepted it, and identified themselves and their colleagues with the agency which was actually bringing the religious era of human history to an end and inaugurating a non-religious rational era. Actually, however, their polemical attitude towards religion was too violent and one-sided to have received support from any such theory of its place in human history. For them it was a thing devoid of all positive value whatever, it was just sheer error, due to the unscrupulous and calculating hypocrisy of a class of beings called priests, who, they seem to have thought, invented it to serve as an instrument of domination over the mass of men. Terms like religion, priest, Middle Ages, barbarism, were for such persons not historical or philosophical or sociological terms with a definite scientific meaning, as they were for Vico, but simply terms of abuse: they had an emotional, not a conceptual, significance. As soon as a term like 'religion' or 'barbarism' has a conceptual significance, the thing that goes by such a name has to be regarded as something with a positive function in human history, and therefore not a mere evil or error but a thing with its own proper value in its own proper place. A truly historical view of human history sees everything in that history as having its own *raison d'être* and coming into existence in order to serve the needs of the men whose minds have corporately created it. To think of any phase in history as altogether irrational is to look at it not as an historian but as a publicist, a polemical writer of tracts for the times. Thus the historical outlook of the Enlightenment was not genuinely historical; in its main motive it was polemical and anti-historical.

For this reason writers like Voltaire and Hume did very little to improve the methods of historical research. They took over the methods devised in the preceding generation by men like Mabillon and Tillemont and the Bollandists, and even these methods they did not use in a really scholarly spirit. They were not sufficiently interested in history for its own sake to persevere in the task of reconstructing the history of obscure and remote periods. Voltaire openly proclaimed that no securely based historical knowledge was attainable for events earlier than the close of the fifteenth century; Hume's *History of England* is a very slight and sketchy piece of work until he comes to the same period, the age of the Tudors. The real cause of this restriction of interest to the modern period was that with their narrow conception of reason they had no sympathy for, and therefore no insight into, what from their point of view were non-rational periods of human history; they only began to be interested in history at the point where it began to be the history of a modern spirit akin to their own, a scientific spirit. In economic terms this meant the spirit of modern industry and commerce. In political terms it meant the spirit of enlightened despotism. They had no conception of institutions as created by the spirit of a people in its historical development; they conceived them as inventions, artifices devised by ngenious thinkers, and imposed by them on the mass of the people. Their idea of religion as due to priestcraft was merely an application of this same principle, the only one they understood, to a phase of history where it did not apply.

The Idea of History (Oxford Paperbacks, 1961), pp. 76–8.

21 The Historical Philosophy of the Enlightenment

H. TREVOR-ROPER

When the 'philosophical historians' of the Enlightenment looked back at the two predecessors whom they all explicitly acknowledged, Machiavelli and Guicciardini, they saw them across an intervening gulf in which they might recognize one or two isolated allies—a Thuanus, a Davila, a Paolo Sarpi—but no continuous tradition. The 17th century, they would admit, had seen a great growth of erudition; but there had been a decline of criticism. Reformation and Counter-Reformation, the serried, rival tomes of the Protestant Centuriators of Magdeburg and the Catholic annalist cardinal Baronius, had alike opened an era of intellectual regression. Since then there had been a great deal of learned accumulation, but criticism, 'philosophy', had—with rare exceptions—been in suspense. In that field, as Gibbon once observed, there had been 'a century of slumber'; and it was the task of the 18th century to begin again. To Voltaire, the period of the Renaissance appeared as the beginning of the modern world; it was then, he wrote, that the human spirit had experienced, 'comme dans notre monde, une révolution qui a tout changé'; and he recognized Machiavelli and Guicciardini as the only historians worthy to be named since antiquity. Gibbon agreed with him. Machiavelli and Guicciardini, he wrote, 'were justly esteemed the first historians of modern languages till, in the present age, Scotland'—that is Hume, Robertson and Adam Smith—'arose to dispute the palm with Italy herself'.

But if the past had been uneven, the future, it now seemed, would be smooth. Looking ahead, neither Voltaire nor Gibbon feared that the intellectual revolution which they had witnessed or helped to make might be reversed. The break-through had occurred. The arts, wrote Voltaire, once established and protected by national independence, cannot be extinguished: they will always spring again. The gains of science, wrote Gibbon, are permanent: no temporary eclipse can stay the progress which they ensure. And amongst the arts and sciences thus permanently established, they saw their own achievement: 'philosophical history', 'critical history', 'universal history' had come to stay.

What was the 'philosophic history' of the Enlightenment, and how is it to be distinguished from the historiography of the 17th century, the century of Bossuet and Maimbourg and Fleury and Tillemont, of the Bollandists and the Maurists, and indeed from the historiography of the 19th century, the century of Ranke and Macaulay and Michelet, of the *Monumenta Germaniae historica* and the Rolls series? The broad lines are clear enough. The 'philosophical' historians rejected the mere accumulation of detail and fact. They also rejected splendid examples, the Plutarchian heroes so popular since the Renaissance. Instead they looked for explanation. In this they had predecessors, of course; but unlike those predecessors they altogether rejected theological explanations. Theological explanation had already been undermined by the 17th century sceptics: the 18th century historians threw it silently overboard and loud was the cry from those who saw it going. . . .

But this was only the beginning. Because they rejected all such theological explanations, the philosophical historians also, by a necessary consequence, rejected any theoretical predilection for Europe or Christendom, and refused to confine the course of history within the time-honoured channels so deeply dug and so faithfully watered by so many Christian writers. In particular, they took a malicious pleasure in devaluing a certain intolerant, insanitary and superstitious tribe which had arrogantly claimed a disproportionate place in the unfolding of the divine plan of human history, the Jews. How absurd it would seem to a civilized Chinaman, exclaimed Voltaire, if he were told that a certain bishop at the other end of the Eurasian landmass—he was referring, of course, to Bossuet—had written a 'universal history' which made no reference to China at all, but deduced the whole course of humanity from the parochial bickerings of those fanatical barbarians! Once god, and his whimsical preferences, had been removed from historical causation, all humanity came naturally and equally in, and most of the great 18th century historians—Mosheim, Voltaire, Robertson, Gibbon—extended their range to other continents and other civilizations, from whose material they impartially drew their conclusions. They believed mankind to be everywhere essentially the same, subject to the same laws, and capable of comparative treatment, even in religion. Finally, having thus rejected the old philosophy of history and widened their field of study, the 'philosophical historians' looked for a new philosophical content. To reanimate the mass of historical *data* into which the old ideological structures had decomposed, they put forward two new concepts whose acceptance may be said to have created the positive historiographical revolution of the Enlightenment. These new concepts were the concept of the organic nature of society and the idea of progress.

Of course these ideas did not explode suddenly upon the intellectual world of Europe. The more we study the roots of any intellectual revolution, the longer and more complex they always turn out to be. The 18th century Enlightenment grew slowly out of 17th century heresy— out of the Arminianism, the Socinianism, the Libertinism, the Quakerism, the Platonism, the Pietism which, in the gradual disintegration of dogma, had merged in undenominational deism. The way for it had been cleared by the scepticism of Bayle and Le Clerc; the new motivation was supplied by the ideas of Locke and Newton. Out of this great intellectual change of the 17th century, the idea of progress gradually and naturally disengaged itself. Long before it was made explicit, it was implicit in the attack of the 'moderns' upon the 'ancients'. If, by 1700, the 'moderns' could, in Mr Willey's phrase, look back on the sages of antiquity from an eminence as lofty as their own, it was clear that the old idea of a golden age, perhaps even of the fall of man, was out of date. Already there had been progress. What had begun could be continued; and the function of history must be, at least in part, to trace the stages by which it had come.

Similarly the idea that human societies have an internal dynamism, dependent on their social structure and articulation, was not new. It had been held by Machiavelli, varied and documented by many of their successors. The great legal and institutional writers of the 17th century, Grotius and Pufendorf, had given it substance; and Grotius and Pufendorf were among the cherished masters of the 'philosophical historians' of the next century. In fact it was because the ground had been so well prepared that the intellectual revolution of the 18th century, when it came, was so complete. Within two years the two new concepts which lay at its base, and had already penetrated men's minds, were made explicit. In 1748 Montesquieu published his great work *De l'esprit des lois*. In 1750 Turgot, in his *Discours* to the Sorbonne, traced the concept of progress in history. Thereafter the great works of 'philosophical history' appeared, precipitated if not originally inspired by these two ideas: Hume's *History of England*, Voltaire's *Essai sur les mœurs*, Robertson's *Charles V* and the *History of America*, and, greatest of all, Gibbon's *Decline and Fall of the Roman Empire*....

Thus, in the third quarter of the 18th century, the revolution in historical studies was completed. Montesquieu had declared the principles on which historians should work, Turgot had suggested the thread they should pursue. History was no longer to be 'a dull chronicle of speeches and battles'; it was to be, as Giannone had urged, *storia civile*, a history of society. Montesquieu himself (we know from his notebooks) had contemplated writing an *Histoire civile de France* comparable with Giannone's *Storia civile di Napoli*. 'Civil history' meant the explanation of social change, illuminated, as Gibbon wrote, by 'criticism and philosophy'; and it was to show, as Voltaire and Robertson showed, the progress of mankind: 'si vous n'avez autre chose à nous dire,' wrote Voltaire, 'sinon qu'un barbare a succedé à un autre barbare sur les bords de l'Oxus et de l'Iaxarte, en quoi êtes-vous utile au public.'[1] How completely these views were accepted can be seen by comparing the greatest works of 'philosophical history' written after the death of Montesquieu: Voltaire's *Essai*, Robertson's two dissertations, Gibbon's *Decline and Fall*. In all we find the same basic assumptions: that history is universal; that its course, though it may be affected in detail by human decisions, is fundamentally determined by the structure of society that is (in Robertson's words), by 'the division of property, together with the maxims and manners to which it gave rise'; that such axioms enable a science of history to be developed and the mechanics of progress to be identified; and, moreover, that this science itself supplies new evidence to the historian. Mere literary evidence, though contemporary, is devalued if it lacks what Voltaire called *vraisemblance*, that is, as Hume and Gibbon applied the concept, if it is incompatible not only with *bon sens*, but with the necessary consequences of economic or social facts. And to all these writers the significant substance of history is the same. The improvement of wealth, the discovery of useful arts, the elaboration of industrial technique, and the creation and preservation of appropriate social institutions are of more interest to them than dynasties, wars, or what even the clergyman Robertson described as 'those uninviting studies' of theology which had consumed so much of the intellectual activity of unenlightened ages.

From 'The Historical Philosophy of the Enlightenment', *Studies on Voltaire and the Eighteenth Century*, vol. 27, (1963), pp. 1668–76.

Perspectives

Whether praised or blamed, the Enlightenment has generally been accepted as an important turning point in intellectual history. Those who praise see it as a moment of release from superstition and bigotry, those who blame, as a fount of new rationalist superstitions and new political bigotries. Looked at more closely, it might seem difficult to isolate the novel elements in Enlightenment thought. This is true if we take faith in reason to be its *point de départ*. In at least one of its many meanings, this faith is as old as the natural law tradition of Thomist and even of Stoic thought; and it was in the seventeenth century that rationalism was given its most substantial and sophisticated metaphysical formulation. It is true also if we take belief in the scientific method to be the Enlightenment's central article of faith. For, even if we discount the claims of other ages, of the Greek or medieval worlds, to be periods of scientific advance, the eighteenth century has little to offer to balance the achievements of Copernicus, Galileo, Bacon and Newton. Yet it is not possible to dismiss completely the age's own claim to originality or the accepted view that it was a decisive stage in intellectual development. The originality is one of mood rather than doctrine. It lies not so much in what was preached as in the fervour of the preacher and the beneficial effects expected of the sermon. What distinguished the Enlightenment above all was its determination to subject all received opinions to the test of reason, to apply this test especially to views on human behaviour, to ethical and political theory, and to extract from the knowledge thus won whatever could be useful in improving the human lot. The mode of thought might have been abstract and derivative, but the fields to which it was applied were virtually untilled and its aims were eminently practical.

Certainly many interpreters have seized on the social and political consequences of the movement as its most significant aspect. And it is no coincidence that interest in and criticism of the Enlightenment has often been triggered off by political events. The French Revolution stimulated the romantic reaction and the Russian Revolution has also brought its harvest of rebukes. Talmon as much as Maistre sees the *philosophes* as primarily creators of a revolutionary ideology. In some ways this is odd, for it was precisely in the area of social and political theory that they were least coherent and least agreed. Yet, in another light, it is not surprising, for the insistence that man and his social environment are subjects of rational inquiry and reconstruction, even if it did not lead to any agreed political programme, was in itself a novel and potentially explosive political attitude.

It was this attitude, this mood, that the Enlightenment bequeathed to the modern world. Its specific philosophic, psychological and political doctrines are now mostly discarded. Both the equation of philosophy with scientific investigation and the attempt to reduce epistemology to psychological description, which was one product of this equation, have long since been abandoned. We can no longer believe that all questions about the mind can be answered empirically and we can no longer follow the sensationalist psychology of the eighteenth century. It is not now easy to accept that there is some demonstrably infallible formula for guiding us in choosing between the varied ends that men can pursue in society. Nor is it possible to admit that problems of social and political analysis can be solved solely in terms of individual psychology. So much has been rejected; yet much has been retained, most notably that men can achieve knowledge of themselves and their society and that they can improve their conditions through the use of organized intelligence and political action.

The twentieth century has seen movements which have denied all that the Enlightenment stood for. Fascism, with its anti-intellectualism, distrust of free inquiry and glorification of violence, stands at the opposite pole. It has seen too the destruction of many of the more flamboyant hopes of the Enlightenment. The idea of automatic progress could hardly survive the experiences of this age of total war, the concentration camp and nuclear weapons. Yet the faith in men's capacity to shape their world remains at the centre of modern ideologies.

The dependence of Marxism on the Enlightenment is a theme that is now well rehearsed and need not be restated. The relationship between liberal thought and the Enlightenment is one that perhaps needs more assertion. Much of the controversy on the nature of Enlightenment thought centres on a disagreement about its view of reason and the scientific enterprise. For those who see the Enlightenment as proclaiming proudly and perhaps presumptuously the conquest of final truths, this age can be convicted of pride and all the evils that follow its enthronement. In politics, it can be seen as the precursor of all those creeds which, certain of their possession of truth, have claimed all the total powers necessary to instate it. For those who see the Enlighten-ment as rather committing itself, however confusedly, impetuously and optimistically, to a scientific method, to a particular mode of pur-suing truth, the age is much more tentative and less knavishly absolute, much more piecemeal and less visionary. In this light it can be seen as a precursor of liberal democracy, a precursor not only of the rational liberalism which believes in the possibility of human improvement through conscious and informed (in other words enlightened) organ-ization of man and his environment, but of the liberalism of tolerance, the defence of free inquiry and concern for individual liberty and dig-nity. For the belief, so dear to the Enlightenment, that society is a moralizing instrument, capable of rational reconstruction and requiring rational behaviour, is a necessary element in any liberal philosophy. Men must be rational, actually or potentially, if democracy is to work or if its purposes are to be achieved. Men must be rational, actually or potentially, if one man's liberty is to be compatible with that of others or if the ends of individual freedom are to be reached. Men must be rational, in practice or in prospect, if that vision of society embedded in liberal thought, which seeks to maintain yet harmonize the varied endeavours of men, is to be at all realized.

Further Reading

Texts

Sir Isaiah Berlin, *The Age of Enlightenment* (Mentor Books, 1956) is a useful anthology, mainly of the British philosophers. It has long extracts from Locke, Berkeley and Hume, and is illuminated by Berlin's penetrating comments. A full selection from Newton's writings can be found in H. S. Thayer, *Newton's Philosophy of Nature* (Hafner Library of Classics). There are numerous translations of Descartes' *Discourse on Method*, probably the most easily available being that of Arthur Wollaston (Penguin Classics, 1960). Professor Lough has edited a helpful selection of articles from the *Encyclopédie* (Cambridge University Press, 1954), whilst d'Alembert's *Preliminary Discourse to the Encyclopedia* is available in the Library of Liberal Arts (Bobbs-Merrill Company, 1963). Rousseau's *Social Contract* and the *Discourses* are published in one volume in the Everyman's Library (Dent). An extremely useful and cheap series is *Les classiques du peuple* (*Éditions Sociales*, Paris); in it can be found selections from the works of Voltaire, Diderot, d'Holbach, Helvétius, La Mettrie, Morelly and Rousseau.

General Works

C. BECKER. *The Heavenly City of the Eighteenth Century Philosophers.* Yale U.P., 1959.

E. CASSIRER. *The Philosophy of the Enlightenment.* Beacon Press, 1951.

A. COBBAN. *In Search of Humanity.* Cape, 1960.

L. G. CROCKER. *The Age of Crisis.* Johns Hopkins Press, 1959.

P. GAY. *The Party of Humanity.* Weidenfeld & Nicolson, 1964.

P. HAZARD. *The European Mind 1680–1715.* Penguin, 1964.

P. HAZARD. *European Thought in the Eighteenth Century.* Hollis & Carter, 1954.

L. STEPHEN. *English Thought in the Eighteenth Century.* Hart-Davis, 1962.

Scientific Thought

G. BUCHDAHL. *The Image of Newton and Locke in the Age of Reason*. Sheed & Ward, 1961.

G. C. GILLISPIE. *The Edge of Objectivity*. Princeton U.P., 1960.

E. GUYENOT. *Les sciences de la vie aux XVIIe et XVIIIe Siècles*. Paris, 1957.

D. MORNET. *Les sciences de la nature en France au XVIIIe Siècle*. Paris 1911.

A. VARTANIAN. *Diderot and Descartes*. Princeton U.P., 1953.

Religion

F. E. MANUEL. *The Eighteenth Century Confronts the Gods*. Harvard U.P., 1959.

R. R. PALMER. *Catholics and Unbelievers in Eighteenth Century France*. Princeton U.P., 1939.

R. POMEAU. *La Religion de Voltaire*. Paris, 1956.

Political Thought

R. DERATHÉ. *Jean-Jacques Rousseau et la Science Politique de son Temps*. Paris. 1950.

P. GAY. *Voltaire's Politics*. Princeton U.P., 1959.

R. HUBERT. *Les sciences sociales dans l'encyclopedie*. Lille, 1923.

KINGSLEY MARTIN. *French Liberal Thought in the Eighteenth Century*. Phoenix House, 1962.

D. MORNET. *Les Origines Intellectuelles de la Révolution Française*. Paris, 1933.

J. L. TALMON. *The Origins of Totalitarian Democracy*. Secker & Warburg, 1952.

Progress

J. B. BURY. *The Idea of Progress*. Macmillan, 1920.

C. FRANKEL. *The Faith of Reason*. King's Crown Press, Columbia University, 1948.

R. V. SAMPSON. *Progress in the Age of Reason*. Heinemann, 1956.

H. VYVERBERG. *Historical Pessimism in the French Enlightenment*. Harvard U.P., 1958.

Index

References in bold type are to pages on which biographical details can be found.